Bilingual Primary Education in the Western Isles, Scotland

Report of the Bilingual Education Project 1975-81

John Murray and Catherine Morrison

Acair 1984

Published in Scotland in 1984 by Acair Ltd, 7 James Street, Stornoway,
Isle of Lewis

ISBN 086152 036 X

Designed by Acair Ltd.
Printed by John G Eccles Printers Ltd, Inverness, Scotland.

The Research and Development Project in English-Gaelic Bilingual Education in Primary Schools in the Gaelic-Speaking Areas, sponsored by the Scottish Education Department and Comhairle nan Eilean (Western Isles Islands Council) was carried out over two consecutive three-year phases which ended in September 1978 and September 1981 respectively. The reports published in this volume were prepared by the project directors in 1978 (John Murray) and 1981 (Catherine Morrison). After consideration by the Consultative Committee of the project, each report was approved by Comhairle nan Eilean which also approved publication. The Scottish Education Department has approved publication.

While the sponsors of the project both favoured publication of these reports, all opinions expressed — except those otherwise attributed — are those of the authors.

Contents

Introduction

This book is an account of the bilingual education developments that
were introduced in primary schools in the Western Isles during the six
years from 1975 to 1981. It is an interesting, varied and sometimes
amusing account and it is intended for a number of audiences. The views
and observations of many people are included, particularly those of
teachers, but the general form of this dual account rested with John
Murray and Catherine Morrison, the project directors. It was they who
asked me to write this Introduction.

The Bilingual Education Project began within months of the setting-
up of Comhairle nan Eilean (Western Isles Islands Council) and was
therefore part of the Comhairle's provision from the beginning. The
members of the Comhairle's Education Department responsible for this
project ensured that is was given the freedom to develop an identity of its
own rather than being seen essentially as part of the Department. It was
set up in informal premises in Lewis and in Uist and with its gifted staff it
built up a unique position for itself within the educational life of the
islands. John Murray's account of the early days in the former tailor's
shop catches the atmosphere very well.

This very informality of setting indicates the democratic and egalita-
rian style by which the project was expected to link with the small and
scattered primary schools in these islands. Together they were to evolve a
relationship which was one of equals seeking by various means to develop
the best in bilingual educational practice. The project was a mechanism
which sought information and ideas from educators of eminence wherever these could be found and assimilated such ideas into an ongoing
programme of development which was being experienced by the teachers
and the project team.

The project team was given the time and the psychological space in
which to develop its own strengths and skills and allow each member to

feel that he or she was being supported as a person. In turn, the members of the project team worked with the teachers as individual persons, whose needs and feelings were acknowledged and honoured — this being the focal point of development in the project.

Materials had to be developed and methods of curricular planning and implementation had to be clarified, but these were as building blocks provided for the teacher to aid her in becoming a secure and innovative person. Over the years the teacher was encouraged to consider and discuss her own attitudes and classroom activities and this could be nurtured only in an atmosphere of mutual trust. What resulted was a web of stronger and more frank relationships which went beyond the every-day professional concerns.

The reports show how this interaction facilitated consideration of how children develop and learn and of the integral place which the child's language experience has within that overall development. Linked closely with his childhood language experiences is the child's sense of place, and in a strong environment such as the Western Isles the double helix of language and physical setting had to be at the heart of any relevant programme of curricular change.

The kernel of this book is the teachers' accounts of how they themselves had changed as people and how this affected the way in which they related to children and how they helped them to learn. The person-centred approach had chain-linked its way from the project team to the teachers and finally to the children. "I very much enjoy this mode of working," stated one teacher, "where such a great deal of talk and discussion takes place and where children become involved with other members of the community. I feel nearer to the children and feel I have a deeper insight into the way that children learn, and the problems they have" (p 135). Another teacher wrote, "I believe that the crux of the development of skills is the opportunity for discussion. Before, the teacher gave, and the children received. Now, it is the other way round, the children give and the teacher helps" (p 147). A third teacher wrote, "My role now is very different to my role in pre-project days when I stood in front of the class and did the telling. Now my role is to manoeuvre classroom discussions in such a way as to get the children to ask questions . . . to get them interested, to direct them to where they can find an answer to their questions . . . (The) skills they should be trained in . . . skills of researching, skills of recording, skills of experiencing and feeling, skills of interpreting experiences. There are no short cuts" (p 138).

The lay-person could be excused for thinking that this project seemed to be concerned more with education than with Gaelic — as if the two could be separated in this way. A major problem facing the project was that, in the past, Gaelic in education was embedded in a medium-orientated didactic mode which relied largely on reading by rotation. What this project enabled teachers to do was to create a range of experiential situations where each child's ever-extending repertoire of Gaelic linguistic skills was being utilised by him so as to realise these situations. The pedagogic shift was fundamental.

These shared experiences, inside and outside the classroom, often gave rise to such verve and individual human interest that some teachers were at times surprised and almost overwhelmed by the children's need and ability to communicate with them and with each other. One teacher wrote, "After this experience they were alive with enthusiasm about every aspect of the topic. We still had to cover a number of (Gaelic) reading extracts and those were attacked with vigour and enjoyment. By this time their vocabulary, in both languages, had extended considerably and they each had their word and phrase books to help them to express their thoughts and feelings in writing. To begin with, a lot of their writing had been descriptive, now they were producing more creative, expressive material. I was so inundated with Gaelic writing at this time that I felt I couldn't cope . . . I found this topic absolutely excellent as an exercise to bring meaning to something which was part of the children's environment, which was my main aim" (p128).

The sense of vigour and creative energy which characterised the best of the bilingual schooling which occurred within many of the project schools was akin to and on a par with the highest quality of accepted practice in this country. In fact the kaleidoscopic effect of having two languages illuminate virtually the whole range of the children's learning experience gave it a unique quality. The adults and the children gained from being part of it and even the remainder of their formal schooling is likely to do no more than smoor the embers of this early experience. "Of course we are enjoying ourselves," stated a teacher in one of the one-teacher project schools. "We are enjoying ourselves very much — but it does not stop there. We come back to the classroom and we do work which we enjoy doing, our outing to the environment having provided us with lively, exciting, interesting work to do . . . All my old traditional methods of teaching have also disappeared eg. reading round the class . . . dry books that children quite often had no interest in, could not understand, did not have feeling for. Spelling is also taught within the context of the theme being studied. Since a great part of our learning resources are found directly in the community there is no doubt that this has affected and altered the relationship between the school and the community" (pp 138-9).

As the quality of education improved so the demand for more and better materials increased. The teacher quoted in the previous paragraph had this to say on children's books and related materials, "But the situation as regards Gaelic materials has definitely changed since the inception of the project and this has already made a great deal of difference to the children's reading. They are most effective and we get a lot of work out of them. I find that I am consciously now more discriminating in assessing the worth of materials. I assess them in the light of the skills they afford and the concepts I can reach through them. We need more and more material, material of every description" (p 140).

As is clear from the teachers' accounts the meaningful and sustained context within which each theme was developed provided adequate opportunity for language work of the most detailed kind, as it provided a range of opportunities for the learner of Gaelic to apply and improve his incipient skills. The teachers render their own first-hand accounts of how the children increased their communicative competence in both languages by means of this approach. Only the teachers were in touch with the children on a regular basis and the progress made by the children was most apparent to them, though they were often surprised by the pace and quality of the change they saw in the children.

It is a sad fact that parental involvement has not been built into the everyday life of Scottish schools and that their contribution is still largely peripheral. The task of opening out the school so as to give parents an essential role was not within the scope of this project. It would have been of considerable benefit to the quality of learning if bilingual parents were given a more significant part to play in all schools at all times. Parents and other members of the communities involved contributed a lot to the work in hand, but the structure was not altered radically so as to give them a definite place in the whole endeavour. Many parents, therefore, tend to remain as mystified by the bilingual methods used as by other modern methods. There remains the need to explain to parents in considerable detail the intricacies of bilingualism and child development.

Many parents in the Western Isles are determined to bring up their children as Gaelic speakers and while they have considerable success during the child's early years they are frustrated and perplexed by the language shift which takes place after a few years. Parents and others tend to rely excessively on the school as a language agent and tend to blame the school when their child's use of Gaelic declines. It is now generally accepted that the school by itself can do very little to affect the extent to which children use Gaelic as their everyday language. The achievements of this project are meaningful in the wider social context only if the everyday life of the child is strengthened and stimulated by the use of Gaelic in the home and in the media. More than ever before in the Gaidhealtachd, the need for a comprehensive radio service for children — from pre-school to adolescence — is an emergency. Only this can complement the liveliness and variety which the primary schools can provide in their native language.

The problems created by the coming of incomers to live in the Western Isles is considerable for the culture and language of the area. Attempts are now under way to have Gaelic playgroups for learners of the language but the provision of appropriate facilities for the young native Gaelic-speaker is a separate issue.

As far as the bilingual project itself is concerned its work continues in the schools but its own structure and welfare have been affected by vicissitudes in the Comhairle's Education Department as well as by the fluctuating responses of the Scottish Education Department. While some may be perplexed that one of its officials can describe the position of the *Scottish* Education Department towards bilingual education as one of "benevolent neutrality" and that the Department's machinations have resulted in a team of researchers from Stirling University conducting what promises to be an authoritarian and disinterested assessment of bilingual classrooms in the Western Isles, Gaels will be surprised by neither.

But the skills and experience which the project shared with teachers help them to continue the excellent work which is described in this book. Teachers expect the quality and quantity of Gaelic books to continue and publishers such as Acair — which grew out of the project — are there to meet this need. Both teachers and parents will benefit greatly in their work with children if an element of the media can be transformed to give an extensive and lasting service.

As long as teachers encourage themselves to move on from the position described by this teacher, "A few years ago there were gasps of dismay from the children and sighs of despair from me when it was time for Gaelic on the timetable" (p 151), or by a second teacher, "I tried to make it as simple as I could, giving them the Gaelic for various parts of the mill etc, but still I felt I was forcing myself and my words on the children" (p 146), the quality of children's lives in school will have been vastly improved. This project, as realised in many classrooms, has shown how this can be done.

Finlay MacLeod
Shawbost, Lewis
August 1984

First Phase 1975-1978
John Murray

1. Setting up the Project

In 1975, Scotland joined the growing list of countries conducting pilot programmes of bilingual education when, as a result of negotiations involving the Scottish Education Department and Comhairle nan Eilean (The Western Isles Islands Council), it was agreed to sponsor jointly the project now known as the Bilingual Education Project, to run for three years from 15 September, 1975. The Scottish Education Department register listed the project as "A Research and Development Project in English-Gaelic Bilingual Education in Primary Schools in the Gaelic-Speaking Areas" and summarised the proposed research as follows:—

> "It is proposed that a three-man team will work full-time for a period of 3 years on the production of teaching materials and of aids to teachers to facilitate the development of a Gaelic-English bilingual curriculum in a sample of primary schools where the children are mainly from Gaelic-speaking homes. Initially, the work of the project will be directed at P1-3 level, but will later be concerned with the middle and upper primary stages. Teachers' working groups will provide support for the team." (Scottish Education Department 1976)[1]

Financial support for the project from the Scottish Education Department would be about £34,000 in all for the 3-year period, to cover the salaries of the project director and a secretary, travel expenses and to assist with purchase of equipment, books and other materials.

The local authority would second two teachers to work full-time as research assistants in the project team and also make a balancing contribution to the costs of the project. The total financial support including staff and operating costs for the three years would be about £68,000.

1

Because the possibility of such a project, based and operating wholly within a local authority structure and area had not been envisaged, initial administrative arrangements were awkward. Unlike England and Wales, Scotland has no national Schools Council through which educational research grants can be channelled, and it was not possible for the Scottish Education Department to make the allocated grant direct to the local authority or to the project. The money had to routed through an institution of higher learning and in this case Jordanhill College of Education, in Glasgow, undertook to administer the grant. This was highly appropriate as the Vice-Principal of the college, John A Smith, had long been actively involved in trying to improve provision for bilingual children in Scottish schools; also, the college attracted most Gaelic-speaking prospective primary school teachers from the Western Isles because it had a Gaelic Department — the only department of its kind in Scotland. The effect of this arrangement was that the project director and secretary would be employed by Jordanhill College and that the project would have to deal with the Finance Departments of the College and Comhairle nan Eilean, neither of which was very interested in the existence or procedures of the other. In fact the director was never conscious of being employed by the College and this attitude was undoubtedly shared by the College itself; teachers and others in the Western Isles assumed, naturally enough, that the director, like the two research assistants, was an employee of Comhairle nan Eilean of a status a little lower than that of specialist advisers.

The operating structure of the project required a unifying element and a Consultative Committee was established to give broad guidance and counsel to the team as well as to speak for the project to the funding authorities. The committee members in 1975 were:—

John A Smith, Vice-Principal, Jordanhill College of Education (Chairman)
John A MacDonald, Gaelic Department, Jordanhill College of Education
Ronald MacDonald, Director of Education, Highland Region
Angus MacLeod, Director of Education, Western Isles
Finlay MacLeod, Primary Adviser, Western Isles
Murdo MacLeod, HMI, Scottish Education Department
William Nicol, HMI, Scottish Education Department
John Nisbet, Professor of Education, University of Aberdeen
Ronald Richardson, Assistant Principal, Jordanhill College of Education

It was expected that the committee would meet about twice yearly, in the Western Isles.

A director and two research assistants were appointed during the summer of 1975 — although the first time they were to meet as a team was about a week after the project had officially begun. The director, John Murray, had taught for eight years in secondary school and subsequently worked for six years as the first Editorial Officer of the Gaelic Books Council where he gained useful knowledge of aspects of Gaelic publishing. Both research assistants were very experienced primary school teachers, who had in their teaching taken into account the unusual range of opportunities and challenges involved in working with bilingual children. Annie MacDonald had been Head Teacher of Claddach Kirkibost School in North Uist for four years before June 1975, having taught previously in Carinish, North Uist and in Iochdar, South Uist. Catherine Morrison came into the team from Airidhantuim School in Lewis where she had taught for thirteen years. Not until November was the team complete, when Christina MacKay took up the post of secretary, returning from Glasgow as John Murray had, to work in the project.

Had the project in fact been based in an institution of higher learning, life would have been considerably easier for the team in the early days. According to Form RES 2 which the Scottish Education Department issues to grant-holding bodies, "the institution" is responsible for providing office accommodation and services for the research team; one wonders how Jordanhill College might have responded to a request to make such provision in Lewis and in Uist. There was no refuge in RES 2. The local authority made the school in Claddach Kirkibost available for use by the project, but the old classroom furnishings remained and there was no telephone. Those team members to be based in Lewis were left to their own devices to find suitable accommodation by both funding authorities, and without the intervention of Finlay MacLeod (then Primary Adviser), who had been instrumental in bringing the project into being, the team and the project would have been in the most extreme difficulties from the outset. Comhairle nan Eilean was probably unaware of these practical problems and could have done little to help in any case; being a wholly new authority, it was striving to overcome its own accommodation problems. Eventually, the team succeeded in obtaining a three-year lease of two upstairs rooms in Kenneth Street, Stornoway. The rooms had previously been used as a tailor's workshop and much of the furniture and equipment was still in place: nine-foot-long work tables, half a dozen large industrial sewing machines, myriads of pins, needles and buttons and a steam press from which radiated a perplexing network of iron piping. The electricity supply was metered jointly with that of the Evangelical Library and of the China and Glass shop which were the immediate neighbours. There was, however, a telephone.

For the first few weeks, the team used office space in Stornoway kindly made available by An Comunn Gaidhealach and by the middle of October 1975 — about a week after the first meeting of the Consultative Committee — the premises in Kenneth Street were usable, if only partially furnished. And by mid-November, a telephone had been fitted in Claddach Kirkibost.

The decision to operate the project from two centres, in Stornoway (Lewis) and Claddach Kirkibost (North Uist) was one of the greatest risks taken by the team in the early days of the project. It meant that from the outset the team would be separated for most of the time, Catherine Morrison and John Murray being based in Stornoway, Annie MacDonald in Claddach Kirkibost. For Annie MacDonald in particular the decision implied three years of working largely alone, without the support of sustained personal contact with other team members, so that she had to rely on the strength and resourcefulness which she had in plenty. Also, the budget would not stretch to arranging personal contacts between teachers in the northern and southern areas. On the other hand, this decision would bring the project centres into close touch with more schools than would have been possible otherwise; it meant that the project would in effect be operating two groups of schools in parallel rather than one widely-dispersed group, so school visiting and meetings of teachers could be arranged more easily and frequently; and, it was hoped, it ensured that teacher groups preparing material would be able to make it particularly relevant to immediate local needs in a small area.

The first meeting of the Consultative Committee on 7 October, 1975 was principally concerned with formulating the aims, tasks and procedures of the project as well as the evaluation method to be adopted. At this vitally important meeting, the course of the project was set. It was agreed that the broad aim of the project was to introduce and to develop in primary schools a bilingual curriculum for children from a Gaelic background; and that the project should "facilitate the introduction of such a curriculum by preparing and evaluating a wide range of resources, by providing guidance as to the most effective use of these, by generating the necessary enthusiasm among teachers and parents and by disseminating information." (Minute No 1, Consultative Committee).

The principal tasks of the project team, working in co-operation with teachers, advisory staff and others were listed as follows:—

a) to devise situations and activities which will stimulate children to use Gaelic as a natural language for exploration and description of experience;
b) to devise and evaluate a wide range of materials — printed and audio-visual — which will facilitate the development of a bilingual curriculum;
c) to provide in-service courses for teachers engaged in the project;
d) to make materials and findings emanating from the project available to all schools in the area;
e) to inform parents and the community and seek to involve them in the project;
f) to develop and maintain connections with similar projects elsewhere and with other interested agencies.

In its first year, the project would concern itself with primary classes 1-3; the following year, classes 4 and 5 would be included; and in 1977-78, with the inclusion of classes 6 and 7, the project would be engaged throughout the whole range of primary school. It was acknowledged that this rate of growth would place severe strain upon the team and the schools, but it was felt that the necessity to make an impact throughout the primary school as a whole was of paramount importance.

The question of evaluation was discussed at some length at this meeting — and has frequently been spoken about since. The committee took the view that because of the unique nature of the project, because the problems were not well-defined and because of the urgent need for development, an open style of operation was called for. Evaluation should be formative, the principal element being continuous overall assessment which should be carried out by the team and the teachers concerned. In this way, the project could take full account in its strategies of experience gained during its operation and retain the flexibility needed to tackle the massive development task ahead.

It was decided that the project should be introduced in 20 of the 60 primary schools in the area. The selection of schools would be carried out in consultation with the Education Department, which would then invite the schools to participate as "trial schools" in the project.

At the end of October 1975, a letter of invitation from the Director of Education was sent to 20 schools. In deciding upon schools, the project and Education Department officials had taken into account the need to involve a range of schools in terms of location and size, other factors influencing selection being the strength of Gaelic language in each area and the ability of staff to speak Gaelic. The Director's letter of invitation stated that the effect of the school's participation in the project would be "gradual but cumulative, so that eventually the whole school will be involved in what is a fundamental and far-reaching alteration in the use of Gaelic in education." The 20 schools, all of which accepted the invitation to participate, were: Airidhantuim, Back, Breasclete, Knockiandue, Leurbost, Lionel, Shawbost and Uig schools in Lewis; Leverhulme Memorial and Scalpay schools in Harris; Dunskellar, Kallin, Paible and Tigharry schools in North Uist; Garrynamonie, Iochdar, Kildonan and Stoneybridge schools in South Uist; Eriskay school; and Eoligarry school in Barra.

The total roll of these schools was 1,100, amounting to 28% of the total primary roll of the Western Isles. All 20 were rural schools and they ranged in size from the 5-teacher primary school at Back with 130 pupils to the 1-teacher school at Kallin with 15 pupils. Although the strength of Gaelic varied from school to school, a survey conducted in February 1976 revealed that 92% of children in project schools had some knowledge of Gaelic and that only two of the 54 teachers involved had no Gaelic.

For material preparation and wider planning, working parties would be drawn from the staff of trial schools, additional members being co-opted as required for specific purposes. There would be two working parties in the first year, one for Uist and Barra and one for Lewis and Harris led respectively by Annie MacDonald and Catherine Morrison. These working parties would normally meet in the project centres, but smaller groups would meet in schools and "other locations". The working parties would prepare teaching material, and test this in their classrooms; after revision in the light of these trials, the material would be "made more widely available". This neat and somewhat sedate procedure was, of course, laid down before the team had had their first contacts with the schools and teachers.

Fraught as these first few weeks were with practical problems, the team nevertheless found time for very intensive and purposeful discussion, for wide reading and fundamental planning. So much information had to be absorbed, so many roads were open and choices had to be carefully made. Obviously a considerable increase in the use of Gaelic and a great increase in Gaelic materials for teachers and children had to be effected in order to develop a bilingual curriculum. How could such increases be achieved? Could more Gaelic and a change in its use be carried into schools by an influx of printed materials? What kind of materials? What should such materials stimulate, support or extend in the classroom? What values, approaches and methodology should such materials imply, since all teaching material carries its own submerged set of these?

Gradually, through close examination and discussion of questions such as these, it became apparent that in order to achieve the radical change aimed at, the project should have to concentrate first upon the

6

people concerned, rather than upon devising instruments for imaginary persons in notional classrooms. In the case of the children, the degree of continuity or discontinuity between their experiences in their homes, communities and schools would be the critical factor while the teacher's attitude to Gaelic, to education and to the community would regulate in practice the use of any instrument or the effectiveness of any methodology employed by the project to bring about change.

"Education is a continuous process which happens everywhere. The school is only one of many contexts in which children learn. The most important context for learning in the early years is the home. To be effective, the work of the school should build on the work of the home.
Different aspects of children's learning should not be fragmented. The young child cannot readily distinguish between different role systems and behavioural expectations at home and school. School experiences should not be separated off from other children's experiences.
Professional teachers should not view education as their exclusive province, and school as the sole context in which it occurs. They should see a broader role for themselves as facilitating learning wherever it occurs.
. . . Educational planning should be localised and responsive to the community served by the school." (Woodhead 1977)[2]

Underlying all the other aims of the project was the attempt to discover and to meet the special needs of the bilingual child in terms of the local and national communities to which that child naturally belongs. The project's only access to the children was indirectly through teachers. Thus it was necessary first to discover the way in which teachers perceived the children's needs, the teachers' perception of their own roles in school and community. Subsequently the team had to be ready to persuade or to convince teachers that something had to be done, that it could be done and that they were the people to plan and implement radical change.

Thus the project deliberately entered into an area of complex and labile personal attitudes — attitudes to language, to school, to education, to the past and future of the community and the environment. It was agreed that the team should seek to build up good personal relationships with each teacher by frequent individual discussion, that all meetings should be as relaxed and informal as possible to facilitate the development of discourse and that the team should seek to bring latent attitudes of all kinds into the open by encouraging public discussion and debate about bilingualism or bilingual education.

Consideration was also given to the context in which any change would occur. While an increase in the amount of time devoted in school to the teaching of Gaelic in formal language-lesson settings would reduce the time available for other activities — a "minus" in educational terms — the introduction of Gaelic as a medium for teaching and learning would affect the content of the entire curriculum and had to be an educational "plus". This move could not be described in terms of time spent but in terms of what was learned. Thus the project was from the beginning concerned with the primary school curriculum and with curricular change, with the language development of children in primary school. The work done through Gaelic would have to enrich the primary school curriculum as a whole.

In many schools there had been in the past a considerable amount of time spent on Gaelic, but mainly the study of Gaelic itself and the emphasis tended to be on reading and writing: it was not unknown for pupils to be able to read and write Gaelic but not to speak Gaelic. The team agreed that in the first instance, teachers should be urged to concentrate upon oral work, on the development of fluent, spontaneous and varied oral expression. Acceptance of this would imply adoption by teachers of an experiential approach and the team decided at the outset that it should state explicitly the belief that spontaneous oral expresssion would emanate most readily from the personal experience of the child at home, in the natural environment and in school.

In the memorandum "Primary Education in Scotland" (Scottish Education Department 1965)[3] the lengthiest Chapter is that on Environmental Studies and the teacher of primary classes 1 to 4 is urged to encourage the child "to look more closely at his environment, and to help him, through observation and exploration, to isolate, identify and understand the various aspects of his environmental experiences and to develop the language he needs to describe them." While some teachers had taken up this recommendation and had begun to exploit the rich resources of the physical and cultural environment in the islands, there was no general systematic development of such work in primary schools. In most cases, the school classroom remained the only acceptable place for learning and teaching, removed from the ebb and flow of daily life outside.

It was this underdeveloped, potentially exciting and educationally rich area of the curriculum that the project team selected as the principal area in which the desired curriculum change could be effected. The rationale of the project was clear: the principal aim, without which none of the project's objectives could be achieved, was that primary education should be sufficiently flexible and relevant to respond positively to the local environment and community.

This formulation of the aims and methodology of the project in the early weeks took place against a background of urgent practical problems of setting up the two project offices.

The shared vicissitudes also helped to bring the team together. At the beginning of the project Annie MacDonald and Catherine Morrison shared fading memories of teacher training at Jordanhill College; John Murray had never met Catherine Morrison and had seen Annie MacDonald once at a meeting in Stornoway. A few weeks later, they had developed into a flexible, tolerant team aware of individual strengths and weaknesses, predilections and skills. Without this early development, no one of the three could have withstood the extreme, sustained pressures and the increasing public exposure the project was to bear over the next three years. This period of intensive assimilation of information and ideas from a variety of sources was crucially important in placing the team and the individual members of it in a learning set as well as in developing the main thrusts, the pace, method and style of operation of the project.

Two incidents recorded in an early internal project report reflect the dramatic absurdity of the early period.

24 September 1975 in the Kenneth Street, Stornoway Premises
Enter John Murray and Arthur Bate (of the China & Glass shop below) with hammers, wrenches, etc. They manhandle six industrial machines and a very heavy steam press to one end of the room and begin, with some trepidation, to dismantle a complex of pipes and gauges which hangs from the ceiling.
Telephone rings. Messrs Murray and Bate search for the telephone, eventually locating it beneath one of three large tables. John Murray gets down beneath the table, answers phone, proceeding to discuss forthcoming meeting of 7 October with John A Smith, Chairman of the Consultative Committee.

December 1975, Kenneth Street premises
The rooms have been decorated, carpeted, partially furnished. A sign on the outside door in large lettering reads
"PROISECT FOGHLUM DA-CHANANACH."
Knock at door. John Murray goes to greet visitor (teacher, perhaps? educationalist?). Tall man with crumpled parcel under his arm.
J Murray: Feasgar math (*Good afternoon*)
Man (proffering parcel): Am bi sibhse a' càradh bhriogaisean? (*Do you repair trousers?*)

2. First Contacts: November 1975 to January/ February 1976

Encouraged by the favourable response to the Director of Education's invitation to schools to participate in the project, the team set out to visit each school in order to outline the aims and procedures of the project to teachers, to discuss in some detail with teachers of primary classes 1-3 their imminent active involvement in the project and, above all, to establish right away the personal contact upon which the progress of the project would be so dependent. It was agreed that the project director should visit all 20 schools while each research assistant would visit the 10 schools with which she would be working regularly. The whole process took several days, as the schools spanned 5 islands and inter-island travel is not particularly easy, especially in winter. Naturally, the team chose to use Gaelic in all their personal approaches to encourage teachers to do likewise in discussion of their own circumstances, opinions and practice.

These first encounters brought the team into contact with the astonishing, bewildering mixture of uncertainty, contradictory attitudes and practice among teachers that affects profoundly the use of Gaelic in schools. The well-known anglicising force of the school as an institution in the past was evident, as was the fact that many schools were still — possibly unawares — alienating children from their linguistic and cultural background.

"Uniformity of educational provision applied to a country in which there are great variations in life style is certain to lead to an education irrelevant and remote from reality for many people . . . Therefore, the school is particularly out of harmony with those communities that, according to tradition, culture, communications and economy are most distant from the urbanised, industrialised and powerful parts of the country — ie. remote and sparsely populated areas." (Høgmo and Solstad 1977)[4]

Teachers all too often switched the conversation to English. In the Lewis and Harris schools, the prevalence of English speaking among teachers in class, in corridor, in playground and in the staffroom was particularly noticeable, though they themselves seemed unaware of it or of its effect upon the children. Outside school, most of them would use Gaelic as the natural language. When teachers express, in English, grave concern about the decline of Gaelic, place the blame for this firmly upon the children's parents and leave it at that, the unfortunate listener is entangled in a maze where the potential for change is difficult to find.

Generally, the project was seen as a *Gaelic* project and the idea of increasing the use of Gaelic was favourably received, especially for the lower range of primary school. Throughout the schools, some time and effort was being devoted to the teaching of Gaelic, usually in a formal "language lesson" style based upon the few available textbooks and often contrasting sharply with the teacher's approach to the teaching of English. The variety of approach, of goals and of achievement was remarkable. Some schools concentrated upon literacy, teaching all pupils — whether Gaelic-speaking or not — to read and write, if not to speak fluently. Others concentrated upon reading but did not teach writing of Gaelic. Many teachers did not seem to know what they were aiming for, and in all schools, English was taught first — beginning in the first week in some cases — regardless of the child's linguistic ability or background. A number of teachers were worried about their own capabilities in Gaelic, doubting that they could operate in a bilingual mode since that would make much heavier demands on their Gaelic than the existing method which was comparatively confined and safe.

There was much questioning, as there still is, about organisation. Composite classes are the norm in the Western Isles as in many rural areas and in all but a few of these there are some children who do not speak Gaelic. How could a bilingual curriculum be followed? Should the non-Gaelic children be included? If not, would everything have to be done twice over? What if non-Gaelic parents objected to the school teaching Gaelic to their children? The project team could not, of course, supply ready answers and would not have done so in any case, an important function of the project being to raise and clarify questions and to encourage teachers to seek out their own answers. This was seen by some as a failing in the team and the attack followed swiftly: *what are the*

11

children going to sacrifice if they get more Gaelic? how can you teach Maths in Gaelic? what about Geography? The majority of teachers, though, looked forward to being able to discuss and explore these problems with their colleagues at meetings, to tell how they tackled them and try out the suggestions of others.

Since teachers were not given any training to work in bilingual schools and communities, neither the questions nor their eagerness to discuss them should have been in any way unexpected or surprising. Colleges of Education in Scotland simply ignored the fact that in a bilingual community, the teacher has a particularly important part to play and that teaching of bilingual children involves a special range and variety of difficulties and opportunities.

The idea of using the natural environment, the daily round of activity and other aspects of the school's surroundings as curriculum material met with general approval. Some schools had been doing this anyway and those which were not or had only gone out very occasionally for special reasons, declared their willingness to try. When contact with *people* as well as birds, animals and inanimate objects was suggested, the response was much more cautious and guarded. One memorable comment on such an approach was that it was no more than "gallivanting about when they should be in school", while another teacher opined that there was little value in environmental studies in "a depressed community such as this."

The project itself and bilingual education were not understood very well. To some, it was a package in preparation, which they would receive in due course; to a few, it was a threatening cloud which would upset their teaching, an additional burden to be borne. Interestingly, it was often seen as something separate from the school and its normal concerns. Comments such as "You have some work to do!" and "Best of luck with your project" epitomised this view. Even a year later, one teacher asked, "Is this project something to do on Friday afternoons?" and in 1978 the head teacher in one school asked a team member, "How is the project doing here, then?"

The team emerged bruised but not too discouraged from this intensive round of initial discussion. The reception had rarely been hostile, rarely enthusiastic; teachers were wary and cautious. It was very clear that a school's acceptance of the invitation to participate did not necessarily mean that all individual teachers — or any of them, in some cases — were keen or willing to become agents of change, even when they themselves considered that change to be desirable. These reactions were expected. The project was, after all, asking teachers to examine the role they played, to examine their own attitudes to Gaelic, to begin to define and to redefine their position in a way that was bound to affect their teaching as a whole, beyond the limits of direct involvement in the project and to have repercussions upon their social lives in the community. It was not a proposal to be accepted lightly. It could, however, be rejected lightly because no professional nor social embarrassment attached to lack of proficiency in Gaelic.

These first contacts confirmed that the project was principally involved in adult education, that access to the children and to the curriculum depended almost wholly upon the team's ability to influence teachers. It was also confirmed that personal relationships would be crucially important for the project and that great skill and discretion would be necessary in order to gain the confidence of teachers while urging them to become self-critical and more resourceful, willing to take up highly exposed positions in their schools and communities. It was also clear that unpredictability and uncertainty were at the heart of the venture, that the team would have to accept this or lower its sights.

While the memories of this round of visits were still fresh and teachers' comments still reverberating in their heads, the project team travelled to Glasgow for discussions with staff at Jordanhill College of Education. After a meeting with staff of the Gaelic and Primary Methods departments, it was arranged that six final year students should carry out teaching practice in schools where the project was involved. While the team would take no responsibility for reporting on students to the College, they would keep in close touch with them during this period and inform them about the project. The College would co-operate with the project team to ensure that these young teachers were aware of the kind of work and the methodology used in the schools. This was the first move on the project's part to alter the training of teachers and it seemed to show great promise as a first step to ensuring that teachers coming to work in bilingual schools had received training appropriate to the task.

The first meetings with teachers of Primary classes 1-3 were scheduled for January 1976 and in view of the generally favourable reaction to the idea of using direct exploration of the environment as a stimulus for development of oral expression, the team continued to assemble reference material, equipment and other supplies to help the teachers to undertake this important first step. The team was still at this stage thinking in terms of "working parties" which would meet to discuss ways of tackling an agreed theme, develop the theme with their own classes and take account of this in further meetings where appropriate materials would be prepared for testing in the "trial schools" and eventual publication. It was agreed that the main aims of these first meetings should be to create a good social atmosphere since the teachers were quite unaccustomed to such meetings, to initiate discussion about the question of bilingual education in relation to their pupils, to agree upon a theme

13

and to begin to outline a plan of work. It would also be necessary to issue the teachers' diaries and to explain the purpose of maintaining this personal record.

The record of these meetings show that a good beginning was made, in that themes were agreed upon and teachers consented to plan out their approach and meet one week later to discuss their plans. Teachers were dubious, however, about the chance of success: at the meetings in Stornoway, in Claddach Kirkibost and Iochdar some teachers declared that the children had scarcely any Gaelic at all. It is also clear that teachers looked to the project team to suggest the theme and to provide the apparatus and that the team members were uneasy about this. Were these groups working parties? When could they become working parties? Might it be that the neat procedures of "working parties" and "trial schools" were not appropriate?

In a report to the Consultative Committee prepared in March 1976, the director stated that "working party" meetings "would be most effective if used as occasions for putting across to teachers the project's aims and approaches, for encouraging teachers to discuss these in an informal atmosphere with team members and among themselves, for raising the morale of teachers daunted by the broad implications of the project."

During this period, it was decided in the light of experience that each teacher should be involved in group discussion. The team ceased to think of working parties and spoke instead of "teacher groups". Soon afterwards, the label "trial school" was abandoned and the schools became known as "project schools." In retrospect, these proved to be wise re-alignments, bringing the project into phase with the actual rather than the conjectural situation in schools. Further, the formative, strategic mode of evaluation which enabled — indeed, encouraged — creativity of attack was already justified.

3. Development in School

This report as a whole is concerned with giving an account of developments which are rooted in schools and which impinge upon or affect the school curriculum. The focus of this chapter, however, is upon the project in action in the classrooms in the course of three school sessions: from January to June 1976 and the full August to June periods in the two succeeding school years.

The starting point for introduction of bilingual education was the bilingual and bicultural background from which the children came — what the child coming into P1 brought to school. In the previous decade, primary education had been moving towards a broadly child-centred approach:

"The function of the primary school is not merely to prepare (the child) for secondary education or to teach him the basic skills, but to begin to prepare him for life. Consequently it must concern itself with the whole child, fashioning its organisation, its curriculum and its methods in such a way as to cater for every facet of his developing personality . . ."

"In determining the type of education which is appropriate in the primary school, it has to be appreciated that the child grows up in an environment of which school is only a part and that he is exposed to the influence of a great variety of elements — people, places, events and things — which, both before and during his period of primary school, constitute the major part of his waking life . . . Education cannot hope to be relevant to the needs of the child, or to the world in which he lives, unless it takes this environment into account, using

> whatever positive contribution can be derived from it and
> endeavouring to compensate for what it lacks."
> (Scottish Education Department 1975)[3]

However, because the educational system had not in the past considered having Gaelic as one's mother tongue a "positive contribution",
schools had been led to regard strength in Gaelic as weakness in English,
to concentrate upon teaching English and through English from the
earliest stage as a means of compensating children for an imagined "lack"
in their background. Teachers in bilingual areas were themselves educated in this way; their professional training took virtually no account of
the existence of bilingualism. Thus they found themselves in their
classrooms perplexed by contradictory pressures. On the one hand, they
were being asked to practise a relevant, child-centred method; on the
other, they felt they had to teach through English only, to relegate the
stronger language of the child to a language-lesson compound. It is not
surprising that most teachers welcomed the advent of the project as a
structure which might help them to resolve these difficulties.

The project advocated a child-centred, *bilingual* approach and this
required the teacher to assume a role to which most were not accustomed. Teachers of P1-P3 were, of course, accustomed to making use of
Gaelic, of necessity, in working with predominantly Gaelic-speaking
children, but only as a bridge until such time as the children acquired
sufficient English for Gaelic to be abandoned as a teaching and learning
medium. It was important for these teachers to know that this did not
constitute bilingual education as perceived by the project; that the aim of
the project was to produce Gaelic/English bilinguals with a mastery of
the skills of understanding, speaking, reading and writing in both
languages together with an appreciation of the nuances, emotional
overtones and cultural dimensions of the two languages, and that this aim
could be realised only through the concurrent use of two languages as
media of instruction for a child in any given school in any or in all of the
school curriculum except the actual study of the languages themselves.
(Gaarder 1967)[5]

In order that teachers should be enabled to work towards this kind of
bilingual education, they had to have access to support, guidance,
materials and ideas as well as a forum for discussion, debate and
concentrated planning. It was the team's responsibility to provide these
as far as it was able and in so doing to create the conditions which would
facilitate change.

The formation of teacher groups to meet as frequently as possible was
an innovation of the utmost importance for this purpose. Without the

blend of social and professional interaction between isolated colleagues which these group meetings initiated and encouraged, progress would have been haphazard in the short term and the long-term aims of the project inaccessible. For the project team, who over the three years led well over 100 such meetings, each one required much preparatory work as well as sensitive, discreet deployment of a range of skills. Such groups were new in the experience of teachers and the team. Constructive discussion did not happen automatically when teachers were brought together, and at the early stage all groups looked to the project team member to do most of the talking. Gradually, as teachers became familiar with the thinking and practice of their colleagues, these groups began to function well. The role of the project team member throughout was to encourage discussion of the curriculum — to provoke it, sometimes — to listen carefully, to seek to elucidate problems, to encourage the group towards an agreed course of action and above all to maintain a thrust in the direction of the new approach required.

Teachers had to do more than discuss curricular change: they had to attempt to implement new ideas in practical ways with their classes. When the work undertaken by teachers and classes in the project began to appear, it affected group meetings considerably. Through listening to others talking about project work done and seeing or hearing samples of that work, teachers derived fresh ideas, learned new techniques and were encouraged in most cases to try these in their own classrooms. In this way, the project's progress in the school curriculum was based firmly upon the collective experience and developing discussion of teachers. In the course of three years, teachers became conversant with the principal aims and the line of approach of the project, so that they became more independent of the project team. A number of teachers now wish to have more autonomy and this indicates the increasing self-reliance of teachers within the broad approach recommended by the project. At the same time, teachers find group discussion most useful so the project has begun to devise strategies to take advantage of these complementary developments.

The interest of teachers in their colleagues' work led the team to organise small group meetings in schools. Because discussion focussed on the work of one teacher in her own classroom, more detailed and extended consideration was possible than with the larger group in the project centres. Teachers were able to gain a better understanding of all aspects of the situation in which the work was produced, of the way in which their colleagues organised their teaching, their classes and classrooms. All this, together with the information and advice they obtained from the project team, encouraged teachers to assess their own circumstances, to be self-critical and reflective.

Project team members also visited schools as often as possible for individual discussion with teachers. By becoming very familiar with each teacher in her working environment, the team was able to give more particular attention to that teacher's needs and to keep abreast of the detailed work proceeding in the classrooms: at the end of the first phase, 54 classrooms were involved. In the evolving relationship between teachers and the project team, these visits were of great importance. Initially, teachers felt some unease about unheralded visits and, equally, it was difficult for the project team member to allay this apprehension by means of a quick, neat explanation of the purpose of the visit. The team member had to judge from observation and discussion, not simply the apparent progress with a particular theme or activity, but the context in which the work was taking place and its effect upon all those involved. The number of teachers who welcomed these opportunities to discuss immediate and wider concerns increased gradually as their confidence in the relationship with the team grew. For the team it was essential to be closely aware of the special strengths of each teacher, to respond positively to these and to try to persuade the teacher to develop these in a bilingual mode, by suggesting modifications or fresh approaches, or by bringing equipment and materials. It was a mutual process of clearing space for development, identifying targets, raising aims.

In helping teachers to adapt to the fundamental change that bilingual education required, it was found that no method or technique used was sufficient in itself. Notes of guidance prepared for a particular purpose by the project team as a result of meetings with teachers had to be discussed with teachers in their classrooms, and if the occasion demanded, the team member had to be prepared to take the class to demonstrate some of the potential of these notes. The inherent danger in taking demonstration lessons was that the team should come to be regarded as itinerant teachers, permitting only a passive involvement on the part of the teacher. The team, aware of this risk, used the "demonstration" approach very sparingly.

At the beginning, teachers agreed that there was a need to stem the steady decline of Gaelic. Many asserted that their pupils spoke little Gaelic, that what Gaelic the children had was of a debased, impoverished standard and that anything the project could do to remedy this condition would be welcomed. The project was seen as a source of more and better Gaelic books and teachers were willing to co-operate with the team in preparation of these. The project certainly aimed to produce books and other materials but these had to be devised and constructed to facilitate the teaching approach advocated by the project. The appropriate form and content could only be ascertained through a close involvement with children in schools, through work carried out by teachers as part of their

18

activity in the project. Thus the project could not plunge into preparation of materials. The essential first step was to inform teachers of the rationale of the project insofar as it was then formulated. Only then could the nature of the appropriate materials be delineated and the processes by which they might be developed. In these processes, the role of the teacher was the crucial governing factor.

The project team had established that teachers were willing to use environmental studies as the context most suitable for introducing change. Accordingly, at the first meetings, the team suggested themes likely to sustain the interest of children, through which the child's concepts and skills could be developed. The choice of theme was based upon criteria such as its potential for direct, personal experience; its potential for development of sensory and affective awareness; its suitability for the age-group concerned and its relevance to the children's environment. As an integral part of work of any of these themes, teachers took their classes outside to carry out direct investigation of the environment. For the teacher, these excursions provided surroundings where it was much easier to use Gaelic naturally as a teaching medium; for children they provided a familiar background in which they were confident in their approach to fresh experience and in their discussions.

Within a few weeks of starting, the project was beginning to show results in the classroom. Through taking children out and sharing experiences with them, teachers were beginning to discern more clearly the real facility children had in Gaelic. Teachers also found that the more they themselves made use of Gaelic in school, the more children responded in Gaelic. Also, more care and attention was being given to the development of Gaelic oral expression, in particular to skills of discussion. The teacher was thus helping the child to extract meaning from fresh experience and to capture in language the quality of that experience.

These new school situations were seen to be providing for children more incentive for learning. Their enjoyment of the work and their eagerness to talk about their experiences were remarked upon by teachers and by parents. The children began to acquire a new awareness and curiosity about their surroundings — an awareness which was not, of course, confined to the school day. Teachers were also learning more about aspects of the environment, developing new interests. Working and learning through Gaelic was becoming more attractive and rewarding for everyone concerned.

Talking and listening were not the only skills being developed for communication of experience. Children were led to describe their experiences for themselves and for others in various ways — through writing, drama, painting, modelling and so on — and to make use of simple cameras, tape recorders, slide-viewers, listening centres, etc., as tools for recording their special view of the world. As the months advanced, classroom walls displayed a changing array of colourful friezes, paintings and photographs with stories and captions in Gaelic. The scope, variety and exuberance of the work indicated the enthusiasm with which it had been tackled, as well as the way in which teachers adapted their skills to the new situation. Recording in these ways was not an end in itself. With guidance and encouragement from the teacher, children analysed, interpreted and drew conclusions from what had been recorded insofar as they were able and so derived maximum benefit from their shared experience.

> "We have discussed the kind of approach which we believe will produce the language development we regard as essential. This involves creating situations in which, to satisfy his own purpose, a child encounters the need to use more elaborate forms and is thus motivated to extend the complexity of language available to him. It also involves the teacher in charting the process by careful observation of the developing language skills." (Bullock 1975)[6]

Children also had to develop the necessary skills for writing in Gaelic. The kind of work undertaken, the freeing of Gaelic from its previously restricted area of operation and the developing interest of children in writing in Gaelic, brought out very clearly the comparatively scant attention generally given to this in the past. The need for systematic help with spelling had not arisen and, in general, the children's skill in writing was not nearly adequate to cope with their aspirations. Often, the results of their efforts in Gaelic were unintelligible to others and completely out of phase with their writing capability in English. This created problems and frustrations for teachers who did not have recourse to a choice of systems or remedies as they would for English. The project team with the co-operation of teachers began to experiment with various ways of improving the performance of children in spelling Gaelic.

At an early stage children were encouraged to circumvent their lack of technical skill by dictating to the teacher what they wanted to write — a sentence or two about their own drawings, or labelling of items. By this method where the content was controlled by the child or a group of children, fairly lengthy stories and short illustrated booklets were compiled. In the process, the teacher occupied a most challenging and influential position intermediate between the child and the child's desire, between the children's knowledge of language and their skills in writing.

In discussion of early writing and reading the project team and teachers were particularly fortunate that David MacKay, who had directed the project which led to publication of the scheme "Breakthrough to Literacy" (Schools Council Publication 1970)[7], was in the islands to lead the feasibility year of the Community Education Project. His work in a project set in a bilingual community in the Caribbean had given him experience of similar problems related to child development and curriculum innovation. By means of in-service courses, teachers' meetings, seminars and frequent informal discussion, he contributed greatly to developing the thinking of the team and the teachers. To the team — and to several teachers — it had seemed from the beginning that the approach and techniques of the "Breakthrough" scheme were of especial relevance for Gaelic in bridging the gap between dictating to the teacher and more independent deployment of one's own language resources. After individual teachers had found such a system to work very well, the project compiled from children's work a basic list of about 100 words and held meetings in schools to show teachers the organisation, the potential and the underlying theory of this initial resource. Teachers found that this method was very effective in helping children to express themselves in writing as well as introducing them to reading and enabling them to build up their own bank of written words in accordance with their development.

One of the merits of this two-stage introduction to writing and reading, which appeared to be working well by the end of the first phase, is that children are able to express themselves in correctly-spelt words, in punctuated sentences. Possibly because of the narrow field in which Gaelic was studied and the emphasis upon 'correctness' in the past, it is not uncommon for teachers to regard Gaelic as they know it as a pure form and to regard children's attempts to write freely as too risky — the risk being the disfiguration of an imagined perfect Gaelic. The project had to find a course which would neither alienate nor completely satisfy the teacher whose adoration of Gaelic written form took precedence over assessment of content and at the same time avoid the doldrums of unintelligibility where content dissolved in formlessness. Teachers seeing the remarkable progress made by children in the range and fluency of writing in Gaelic were reassured; the remark "I could never have done that", made by a teacher on seeing a passage written by a child is indicative of the quality of the work emerging from classrooms in the project. During the first three years, great strides were taken in the development of written and spoken Gaelic and this improvement could largely be attributed to the new kind of stimulation children were receiving.

Just as the writing was derived from a base of spoken language and experience, so also reading material was related closely to the children's interests, abilities and feelings. In this way, the reading material had more purpose and meaning for them; they were keener to read and more confident in their approach to reading. The activities undertaken by classes generated a growing body of children's writing, and teachers were encouraged to make full use of this as reading material. Children showed great interest in their classmates' work, not least because the written language in that work was the children's own language. Work which formerly might have been tucked away in individual jotters was now being made freely accessible to all in the form of attractive friezes and booklets.

While there was a great increase in the amount of Gaelic reading and writing done by children with guidance and stimulation from teachers, most teachers continued to insist upon teaching the reading of English first regardless of the relative English and Gaelic strengths of the children. Those who did agree to introduce Gaelic-speaking children to reading through Gaelic found, naturally enough, that it worked well. They also found that these children were much better able to tackle English reading at a later stage from a base of confidence than a base of bewilderment. For most teachers, this request by the project remained — in the first phase, at least — an insuperable obstacle. One can enumerate reasons for baulking at it, such as the utter lack of suitable pre-reading and early reading material, of comics, picture-books, dic-tionaries and so on; but notwithstanding the validity of these, it would appear that an accumulated set of attitudes to language and to education underlie the present reluctance of teachers to introduce this, or of parents to insist upon it. As long ago as 1866, Alexander Nicolson, Assistant Commissioner appointed by the Royal Commission on Education, said in a report on the State of Education in the Hebrides:

> "Many persons, teachers and others, appear to consider the use of the Gaelic language in the school as a mark of rusticity, and think it better that the children be addressed in words which they don't understand, rather than derogate from the dignity of the business by using the vulgar tongue. I think this is a mistake in philosophy and practice . . ."

It is obvious that great advances in the status of Gaelic have taken place since then, but a glimpse of the past helps in seeking to appreciate the difficulty faced by teachers in 1976 asked to take a step which they accept as logical, but find almost impossible to undertake in practice. The provision of carefully-designed material for early reading, which formed an important part of the work of the first phase, will help in surmounting this obstacle, as will the deepening knowledge of teachers about the particular needs of the bilingual child and the increasing interest and confidence in bilingual education. For the project, it was supremely important to build upon strength of teachers, to assist them to become more self-reliant in a new situation and to establish structures and initiate processes which are conducive to innovation and planned change.

There was universal agreement about the need to devise a suitable reading scheme for young children and much time was spent in discussion with teachers of the form such a scheme might take. This discussion of an area of seminal importance was itself extremely valuable, enhancing awareness and appraisal of reading material in both languages and bringing up fundamental issues concerning language development. As a result of discussions and of the evident advances being made in Gaelic, it was agreed that the project — children, teachers and team — should try to devise an appropriate scheme. Certain criteria were agreed. The scheme should be flexible, multi-faceted, with many "entry points"; it should develop and grow as did the children's own work in class; it should be based firmly upon the actual language use of children; it should relate closely to the experience and interests of children; it should be imaginative and stimulating; it should be graded on bases which took full account, not only of word length or complexity of statement, but of the conceptual and imaginative development of the child. A daunting task, but the project, working so closely with teachers and their classes was in an unusually advantageous position to undertake it. Accordingly, teachers and their classes embarked upon the theme "Sinn Fhéin" (Ourselves) in 1977 and by the end of the first phase, preparation of the scheme was well under way.

The project continued to work with P1-3 during the three years of the first phase. In the second year, a course had to be set for ensuing stages of primary school; that year P4/5 were included and P6/7 in the third year. In practice, all classes between P4 and P7 were influenced by project work from the beginning of the second year in many smaller schools where one teacher took the whole range. As before, new teacher groups were organised and classroom visiting was extended to include these teachers — as was the case again at the beginning of the third year. Planning of the second year had to take into account the findings of the first as well as the need for appropriate sequential development right through to P7. At this stage, the project had to work out, tentatively, the kind of primary school curriculum which might be aimed at, a programme which would cater for the bilingual child to the age of twelve while augmenting the existing curriculum.

It was agreed with teachers that the environmental bias should be retained at this level, though the definition of environment would be slightly different to take account of the comparative maturity of the children. Various aspects of the environment could now be the subject of progressively deeper levels of study. The children could also reach out to wider environments, though their understanding of these would depend upon confident knowledge of aspects of their own immediate surroundings. It was also agreed that while, on occasion, the starting point would be local study based on direct exploration, at other times the stimulus should come from a work of fiction being read by the class. Fiction used as a centre of interest would serve as a springboard into environmental studies as well as providing scope for imaginative work in both languages.

The extreme shortage of suitable works of fiction in Gaelic presented difficulties, highlighting yet again the very low baseline from which schools had to begin and the ever-increasing, urgent needs with which the teachers and the project team were confronted at every turn. Because the children were bilingual, however, it was decided that English works of fiction should be used, the developmental work being tackled in both languages. Through liaison between the project team and the Schools Department of the BBC, it became possible for classes to read a book in English and have access to a Gaelic adaptation broadcast over several weeks. "Hill's End" by Ivan Southall, which is set in Australia and "Mark of the Horselord" by Rosemary Sutcliffe, a novel about the Picts and Scots were both used in this particular way with remarkable success. By choosing novels of strongly historical or geographical content and extending their use in this way, children were introduced to social studies. Significantly, Gaelic was being used as a medium in the integration of many school subjects and a different approach to the teaching of History and Geography was encouraged.

At this stage of their schooling, children's concept of space and time are immature. Accordingly, emphasis was placed upon the study of Man in his Environment, the changing social conditions and how he adapted to these. As before, the children's own experience formed the basis for such study and the teacher's role was more to guide their explorations than to transmit facts by instruction. The development of skills and of ways of learning were the principal aims, so that the children learned how to learn. Because the work was close to their own experience, children were more keenly involved and were stimulated to seek out information, to make effective use of the banks of facts available and to develop their reference skills in so doing.

Often the information desired was not to be found in books. Gaelic reference books for adults are rare indeed; for children and schools, there is nothing at present. Again, the project used the situation to advantage. Schools made use of the many other sources of reference which are universally available but all too seldom consulted. The classes went out to investigate sites, to examine objects of historical interest, to observe and learn at first-hand with the sensitive guidance of the teacher. This was not introduced as a stop-gap. The acceptance of the environment by the school as an essential component in a balanced, relevant curriculum validates for the children that environment in all its aspects — not least the people, their language and their way of life. It also ensures the development of reference material which is appropriate.

One new skill systematically developed bilingually by the project was that of mapping. At P4 stage, children were introduced to mapping through the making of plans from objects or models. Careful progression was made through to the stages of compiling and reading maps of the classroom and areas of the village, until the children had progressed to the stage of making and reading smaller scale maps. Through practical mapping work done in their own villages children gained much better understanding of the concept of maps. Recording in plan and map form was done for a variety of purposes. It could be the drawing of a scale-plan of a site of historical interest; a map showing distribution of wild flowers in an area; a map showing land use in the village. It was realised there was much more to understanding mapping than just opening an atlas and that relation of the work to the children's environment led naturally into a variety of studies and disciplines capable of development throughout a lifetime. For example, children measuring houses as part of a mapping exercise are encouraged to notice — and to ask teachers and others about — different housing styles, vacant or ruined houses and so on. In islands with a history of emigration, social studies can never be parochial unless they are undertaken only in the confines of the classroom.

4. Materials

The legacy of neglect was nowhere more obvious than in the great dearth of published books and other materials in Gaelic for children to support the development of Gaelic in the home and in schools. In September, 1975, the total number of Gaelic titles in use in any primary school in the Western Isles was less than 50, of which only about 30 had been published since 1969. The range represented by these titles was narrow, the largest single group being elementary structured reading-books and workbooks (20 titles). Only 4 books had been purposely written to encourage the teaching of anything other than Gaelic language through the medium of Gaelic. And the disadvantage was unequally distributed: there were only half-a-dozen titles suitable for upper primary pupils, so that the child who had, with barely sufficient material, acquired basic reading skills in Gaelic was then given no opportunity to extend, develop and enjoy the use of these skills.

Inevitably, in such circumstances, what books were available tended to be overstretched and little consideration could be given to matching of interest levels with reading levels, or to the Gaelic language experience of the pupils in school being in harmony with their experience outside school hours. Teachers faced with many other problems generally found it impossible to counteract the restrictions of such provision. For them as for the children, misgivings about the worth of Gaelic were deepened and it was not uncommon to concentrate upon eking out this meagre ration of printed words in most unrewarding ways, thus reinforcing the pessimism with which the work had been approached in the first place.

How could the project break this circle? The project had no funds to publish books and the very small number of Gaelic publishers, each operating on a part-time basis and seriously under-capitalised, could not be expected to concentrate their resources on such a narrow age range.

It was against this background that the project began its attempt, not simply to increase the number of books and other materials for primary school children, but to bring about a radical alteration in the kind of material produced and an extension of the range across age of readership and nature of contents.

The project adopted several strategies to tackle the problem and to turn the situation to advantage by developing the resourcefulness of individuals and groups. Teachers and pupils, especially at the lower primary stages, were encouraged to devise their own material, developing it through the activity in which they were currently engaged. The project provided various kinds of paper, ektagraphic slides and slide viewers, simple cameras and cassette tapes together with ideas as to their most effective use. As a result, teachers and pupils became adept at compiling their own tape-slide programmes, illustrated stories, posters and so on. Some of this wealth of exciting and attractive material generated in classrooms was displayed to gatherings of teachers on a number of occasions throughout the islands to good effect and as much as possible was collected into project centres in Uist and Lewis when teacher and class moved on to other themes. As a resource for groups and individual authors this growing bank is of immense value. As a reflection of the new techniques encouraged by the project and of the quality of work emerging from a close articulation of Gaelic with the interest and experience of the bilingual child, it is of considerable importance.

The team, individually and as a group, was engaged in devising materials of various kinds throughout, ranging from handbooks and reference work for teachers to films, slides, rhymes and stories for children. With teacher groups, team members prepared, tested, appraised and refined works for classroom use. With informal groups — meeting on Saturdays in the Stornoway centre, guided by the team and furnished with plentiful supplies of coffee and paper — as many as forty poems and a dozen stories could be produced in one day for distribution to schools a few days later. Individual authors and artists were approached and they willingly provided stories poems and illustrations for use by the project, free. In 1976 the Education Department agreed that Andrew McMorrine, an Art teacher at Iochdar school (South Uist) be seconded to the project team for 2½ days per week to assist with illustrative and graphic work. This enhanced the project's skills greatly, especially in production of published works, but also in much more informal materials issued to schools. The flow of original material, especially for younger children, showed clearly that the low level and narrow range of provision hitherto was in no way attributable to lack of creativity among pupils, teachers or the Gaelic community at large. In fact, the team soon had more manuscripts and other "raw material" than it was able to process and distribute. Neither the team nor teacher groups could possibly devote the necessary time to processing all this excellent work.

Originally, the intention had been to develop and devise suitable material with the help of teachers, to pilot this in schools as "trial" material and then proceed to publish thematic curriculum packs. This projected procedure was soon in shreds. It might be suitable in a world of plenty, where the "trial material" is an infinitesimal proportion of the total printed works available, but the project was "trying" water in a desert. It is a credit to the restraint and determination of teachers that the project did, in some cases, manage to follow the "trial" process stage by stage. One could not distribute enough "trial material" in script, type-script or any other form to satisfy the need nor to sustain the continuing development once Gaelic had been given a slack rein in the school curriculum. Also, printed material distributed in this form was unattractive, comparing badly even with English material of inferior quality and strengthening the impression in the children's minds that Gaelic was a "hand-me-down" language. The project had to become involved in Gaelic publishing.

The first book in which the project had a hand was "Tugainn Cuairt" (Let's go for a Walk), published by An Comunn Gaidhealach in 1976. This collection of stories designed to be read and discussed with young children was edited, designed and seen through the production process by the team who also discussed the book with teachers before publication and distributed a leaflet of guidance for its use on publication. A second book similarly processed by the project in 1976 appeared early in 1977 — "Leagsaidh Luchag" (Lexy Mouse), published by Clo-Beag. These books were well received and all concerned were happy at the outcome of this co-operation of author, project and publisher. Following this encouraging beginning, the project co-operated with An Comunn Gaidhealach and the Highlands and Islands Development Board (HIDB) to produce six illustrated books — the *Cliath* series, published by HIDB and An Comunn Gaidhealach in August 1977. The principal role of the project was in originating and editing the series, though in practice team members worked closely with officials of An Comunn Gaidhealach and the HIDB as a group. Three of the books were designed for children up to the age of 7, the other three for 8 to 10 year olds. One of the books for the younger group and two of the others emanated directly from the project, the other three books being contributed by independent authors and illustrated by independent artists.

In preparing these for publication, careful attention was given by the project to selection of typeface, vocabulary range, line length control, complexity of the story and aptness of illustration to ensure that the finished product matched the highest international standards both in appearance and in content. The books were launched in Stornoway and in Balivanich at a teachers' in-service course and distributed to schools at once. Their publication attracted widespread attention from the national press, gaining good publicity for the parties concerned and for the funding bodies of the project as a whole: "Stornoway gets first Gaelic story book for a generation" trumpeted the "Times", from London, somewhat inaccurately.

The funding for the series — amounting to over £6,000 — had been provided by the Highlands and Islands Development Board. Nevertheless the Scottish Education Department advised that copyright be assigned to Jordanhill College of Education, that royalties should be split equally between the College and the Department for the duration of the project, the accrued revenue to be divided thereafter between the authors and the Department. On the insistence of the independent authors that they waived royalties only in favour of the project, the Department agreed that all royalties for the series — a maximum of about £900 — should be remitted to project funds at Jordanhill College to be spent at the discretion of the Consultative Committee.

The foregoing account indicates the many different kinds of difficulty which had to be overcome to achieve something that in the world of English educational publishing would be an event of no particular significance. Undaunted by these difficulties, the team embarked on yet another co-operative venture while the *Cliath* books were still being processed. This time the parties involved were Comhairle nan Eilean, Longman Group Ltd (London) and the project team, who had made a direct approach to Longman Group asking for an opportunity to write Gaelic versions of suitable books due to be printed in the near future. Longman Group offered the team the chance of obtaining at a very favourable price Gaelic versions of twelve books to be published for the first time in England at the end of 1977. Having agreed that the books were well suited to furthering the aims and methods of the project, and after securing specific financial support from Comhairle nan Eilean amounting to £6,000, the team accepted the offer.

Preparation of the text for these books involved continual checking of vocabulary against the writings of young children in project schools and working within the spatial constraints imposed by the original design of each book.

The twelve Gaelic *Spàgan* books were eventually published in February 1978, again to an unusual fanfare of publicity. "Spàgan" was announced, welcomed, reviewed and discussed in the press, on radio and on television; in schools, children and teachers found the books delightful and many amusing and exuberant stories, drawings and models of Spàgan (the amiable central character of the series) began to flow from classrooms. Again, the highest standard of production was matched by extremely careful selection and preparation of content.

While work on the *Spàgan* and *Cliath* series was in progress, the team also co-operated in preparation of Gaelic versions of a series of four books published late in 1977 by Oliver and Boyd. The series, *Blàir Mhór an t-Saoghail*, (Great Battles of the World), presented an opportunity to use Gaelic in new contexts, thus helping to extend its range in schools. It is worth noting that when the newly-published books were placed on a desk in the project office, few people, glancing at them, realised that the writing on the cover was in Gaelic, automatically assuming that brightly-coloured covers with a bold variety of lettering belonged to English publications. Such responses are true indications of deeply embedded attitudes.

Publication of the *Spàgan* books in February 1978 brought the number of Gaelic publications written and/or edited in one year by the project for use in primary schools to 24, an unprecedented level of provision; in the past it was rare for more than 5 books of this kind to be published in a year.

One of the less obvious achievements of the project during this period was the bringing together of established agencies in new ways for new purposes, albeit on ad hoc bases. It was clear that while the ingenuity of the team might bring about other fruitful temporary liaisons, the long-term needs of Gaelic children and teachers demanded the establishment of more permanent structure, a steady flow of material and a channel for publication of original Gaelic works in particular. The project director floated the idea of forming an educational publishing company to a number of agencies during the first half of 1977 and was sufficiently encouraged by the response to initiate discussions involving Comhairle nan Eilean, the Highlands and Islands Development Board, An Comunn Gaidhealach and the project itself. In August 1977 a representative Working Group was set up to explore the possibilities and prepare recommendations. The Group's "Report and Recommendations" was considered separately by Comhairle nan Eilean, the Highlands and Islands Development Board and An Comunn Gaidhealach, all of whom by November 1977 had accepted the main recommendations, which were:—

"(i)   that the four named bodies jointly set up and agree to run in the fashion previously described a company limited by shares with an authorised share capital of £10,000 of which £8,000 will initially be issued and equally subscribed by the four organisations;

(ii) that an appropriate company be immediately formed as previously outlined;

(iii) that the four bodies formally approve the initial contributions and ongoing commitments outlined in the report in respect of themselves and enact the necessary formal approvals to give them effect."

(Report and Recommendations of a Working Group regarding establishment of a new bilingual publishing company in the Western Isles. September, 1977).

The fourth body was to have been the project, but it was found impossible for the project to participate as a shareholder. In December, 1977 the new company, Acair Ltd was announced. Soon afterwards, the Board of Directors met and Acair began the search for staff and accommodation, settling eventually in a refurbished mortuary in Stornoway which it shares at present with the North of Scotland College of Agriculture. At the request of the shareholders, the project director has been chairman of the Board from the beginning, so that the project where the idea of the company originated and which to a great extent the company was designed to serve, does, in the meantime, have a voice in its affairs. The company has also attracted substantial support from the Scottish Arts Council and Grampian Television.

Among the first publications of Acair are "Coinneach" (Kenneth), "O Tractor!" and "An Duine Thàinig a Chunntadh nan Tighean" (The Man who Came to Count the Houses), all of which were edited by the project; the last two were, in fact, specifically written to complement the work of the project in environmental studies.

The development of this long-term provision does not, however, eliminate the immediate and pressing needs of children and teachers, especially in the upper ranges of primary school. The shortage of longer, more complex printed works is extreme; there are no Gaelic works of reference, no books on the history of the area and so on. Printed work emanating from the project naturally reflects the activity and findings of previous years, so that one would expect such works for upper primary to be appearing from 1979 onwards. The task of making good the damage caused by a century of malign and benign neglect by central and local education authorities will take many years and considerably greater allocation of resources than the funding the bilingual education project was given — a total sum equivalent to the price of half-a-dozen trucks.

At an intermediate level between published material and stencilled or photocopied matter, the project has secured the co-operation of the Community Education Project to provide a number of lively books for use in playgroups, nursery units and infant classrooms; in these minimal-text books, Gaelic text is simply overlaid on the existing English. By September 1978, eight of these had been issued and a further eight were in the final stages of preparation. The two projects, working with the Music Department and pupils of the Nicolson Institute, BBC Schools (Gaelic) and Noel Eadie of Tong Studios in Lewis, are also engaged in producing recorded cassette tapes of songs with accompanying printed matter for young children.

Reference is made in the preceding chapter to the development of early reading materials in Gaelic, based closely upon the needs, vocabulary and interests of the young children themselves. The absence of a satisfactory modern reading scheme and of suitable printed work for very young children was alleviated to some degree by the approach and techniques encouraged by the project. In 1977, as a result of several meetings and discussions with David MacKay and with P1-3 teachers, it was agreed that the theme "Sinn Fhéin" (Ourselves) should be explored with P1-3. Teachers would seek to assemble on tape and in writing a fairly comprehensive collection of subjects of special interest to the children, of stories and of the language use of the children. As before, by this means, a wealth of material was produced and this formed the basis for a vitally important continuing development of early reading material.

The development of the material is best summarised as stages:—

1. Children produce pictures and stories which are kept or recorded.
2. Teacher groups in workshop sessions sift through the material and devise stories in line with the children's work.
3. The project team fit these stories to a standard format for production: 16pp booklets with one or two lines of large type at the bottom of each page, the rest of which is blank.
4. The books printed in this way are returned to schools for trial by teacher with the children and for the children to illustrate.
5. The books are returned to the project offices, and teachers' comments upon them. In some cases, children alter the story as they go!
6. A further exercise in synthesis, involving the team and teachers, takes place.
7. The final version of the text is printed with illustrations by children or based upon those of the children.
8. The finished book is distributed.

By the end of the first phase of the project, well over 20 such stories were at various stages of the process, 6 being at the stage where final illustration was being carried out. As always, the main difficulty is that of achieving the printing and publication of books with colour illustration: the costs are prohibitive. Nevertheless, the project is continuing with this process rather than opting for an insufficiently comprehensive or relevant reading scheme, because it involves children and their teachers directly in its preparation. The aim is to reduce the project team's involvement gradually so that teachers — given appropriate support and technical back-up — will themselves produce this flow of material which can respond immediately to the changing interests of children.

Another major resource was developed jointly by the two projects together with I Stewart Angus, a marine biologist from Stornoway. The complete resource comprises three main groups of material relating to the natural environment of the seashore. For every school in the Western Isles an authoritative, detailed survey report on a rocky and a sandy shore near the school with safe access (these shores being chosen by schools) was compiled. There is a general introduction and guide to the Hebridean seashore with a comprehensive identification section. In addition, Stewart Angus, a skilful photographer, prepared a central bank of about 600 colour slides, subdivided into six categories: birds, plants, geology, shells, rocky shore animals and sandy shore animals. A classified catalogue of the slides completes the basic resource. By September 1978, preparatory work was virtually complete and those involved were addressing themselves to questions of replication, publication, distribution and organisation of the material, which will be suitable for top primary and early secondary school pupils. Preparation of this work originally began in December 1976, when Stewart Angus, then attending Aberdeen College of Education, accepted the suggestion by the project director that he should prepare one tape/slide programme on seashore life for use in project schools.

From the outset, the project encouraged the use of photography as a means of recording and as a stimulus for discussion. Schools made extensive, effective use of the simple cameras (the "bilingual camera" as one teacher put it) issued by the project, the pupils in many cases taking the photographs and compiling booklets or wall displays. The team, determined to exploit the potential of cine film, obtained the necessary equipment in 1976 and learned some of the basic techniques of filming and editing with the help of Mr J D Beal of Jordanhill College. Annie MacDonald, a highly proficient and experienced photographer, soon learned to use the cine camera skilfully; the other two team members are still at "beginner" stages. Some teachers used the cine cameras to make their own films and pupils enjoyed contributing shots, but the time-lapse between filming and viewing the edited film was found to limit the usefulness of "home-made" cine films. Nevertheless, this activity will be continued because the medium is so powerful. On one occasion in Uist during an exhibition of project school work the project team, on an impulse, screened two or three short films which had just returned from processing for a roomful of secondary school pupils and teachers. Everyone sat down and watched these silent unedited films, utterly absorbed. Twice. The novelty of seeing one's own people and one's own environment as the only content in a film rather than as the decorative background to romantic and travel films transfixed that audience.

The team attempted to use for photography a strategy similar to that for printed works: encouraging schools to develop their own material geared to their own particular needs and at the same time seeking to secure publication through other agencies of high-quality finished work based upon and contributing to the aims and practice of the project. Early in 1976, discussions with the Department of Education at Stirling University began and by May of that year plans had been formulated for the joint production of video cassettes dealing with environmental studies for primary schools. A joint application by the University and the project to the HIDB for financial support was successful and the filming began in June. The children of North Uist schools were filmed as they explored with their teacher various aspects of the surrounding country and carried out preparatory and follow-up work in the classroom. To all concerned, it then seemed that the video cassettes would be ready for distribution in 1977: four cassettes, dealing with the seashore, the birds, flowers and plants and one more general film. It soon became apparent that more filming was needed, other snags cropped up, and the venture began to demand of all concerned the stamina to see it through as a longer term exercise. Fortunately, Annie MacDonald was able to organise, with teachers, the content of much additional film and then to carry out the actual filming. Final editing of the first film was in progress in September 1978. The University staff involved, the project team, pupils, teachers and parents who have seen roughly edited film are confident of the value of the series; the reaction of schools in general remains to be seen. Because of the very time-consuming nature of this enterprise in a busy, crowded project, the effectiveness and the value of the finished product will be carefully monitored by the team.

The BBC appointed a Gaelic Schools Radio Producer shortly before the project began and contact was established with her at once. The provision of Gaelic programmes for schools was a new venture for the BBC which proposed to broadcast two series of twenty programmes each per year: *Culaidh Mhiogais* for early primary classes and *Co Iad?* for the upper primary. These programmes represented an important increase in the resources available for teachers and it was mutually beneficial to work closely together. The extent of this co-operation in practice is described in Chapter 6, but it is relevant here to record that poems, songs and other items have been contributed to programmes by the project, as well as posters for schools to accompany programmes in the *Co Iad?* series.

In 1977, Grampian TV began to broadcast *Cuir Car*, the first Gaelic children's television programmes in the history of broadcasting. By this time, the project was becoming well-known and was receiving offers of co-operation and Grampian TV asked the team to assist in provision of suitable material for inclusion in a forthcoming series. As a result, a film crew spent a week filming children in project schools in their classrooms and outside discussing their work, acting and singing. The schools involved were all in Lewis, because Grampian TV could not be received in the islands south of Lewis at that time. The resulting programmes generated a great deal of interest and it is hoped that further co-operation will take place in the future.

In terms of material development and production, it is difficult to imagine what more the project could have achieved in three years; and the generation by the project of a publishing company which will serve the needs of school children as well as those of the wider community is itself of considerable significance. At least as important as these products, however, is the initiation by the project of new processes, new practices for the creation of classroom material, printed and audio-visual.

5. The Project Reported

PART ONE: The Teachers' Account

Sixty teachers were involved in the first phase of the project. Seven of these teachers left the project schools before the end of the first phase. The remaining 53 teachers were interviewed individually in their schools, once the first phase had been completed. The structured interviews were conducted by Mr Iain MacIver, an Educational Psychologist with Comhairle nan Eilean, and Miss Catherine MacDonald, Lecturer/Tutor in Bilingual Education with Comhairle nan Eilean and Aberdeen College of Education. The interviews were recorded on tape.

Teachers were asked to compare the present performance of children with that of children of the same age of whom they had had experience before the project began. Such questions were not applicable to recently appointed teachers who had not been teaching before the project started. Teachers were assured that neither their own names nor the names of their schools would be disclosed.

THE INTERVIEW SCHEDULE

1. *You have been with the project for how many years now?*

Table 1

	3 years	2 years	1 year
No of teachers	21	19	13

2. *In general, have you enjoyed being in the project, or would you be glad to see it finished?*

Table 2(a)

	Enjoyed Project	Did not enjoy Project	N/A (No answer recorded)
No of teachers	45	3	5

Table 2(b)

	Glad to see it finished	Not glad to see it finished	N/A
No of teachers	3	14	36

It is clear that most of the teachers enjoyed being in the project. Having stated this in the first part of the answer, it would seem that few of them thought it necessary to answer the second part of the question. The same three teachers who disliked being in the project said that they would be glad to see it finished.

Comments — "I enjoyed taking part in it for the most part. Some of the things I found a bit difficult to begin with, but I have enjoyed it all."

— "Now that it's here it has become part of the curriculum and part of our work and I can hardly see it as an isolated thing."

— "I've enjoyed being in the project, but I've felt that we've had too much pressure on us to produce results."

— "I have enjoyed parts of the project. I wouldn't be glad to see it finished if it means an end to the aims and ambitions connected with the project. I wouldn't like to see that ended at all. I'd like it continued and extended."

3. *At the beginning of the project —*
   (a) *Did the project seem a good idea to you?*

Table 3 (a)

A good idea	Not a good idea	N/A
37	10	6

(b) *How do you feel about the project now?*

Table 3(b)

A good idea	Not a good idea	N/A
43	3	7

Most of the teachers felt from the start that the project was a good idea, and more of them felt that way by the end of the first phase. The number of teachers who said that they had enjoyed the project (Table 2(a)) is roughly the same as the number who felt at the end of the first phase that it was a good idea (Table 3(b)).

Comments — "I thought it was good idea because I thought something should be done to help the children with their Gaelic. I still think it's a good idea and that it should carry on."

— "No, not at the beginning. This was because Gaelic had declined. Now I feel quite differently about it."

— "I can't say it did seem a good idea. I feel differently now. I think it has some good points."

— "Yes, a good idea.
I still think it's a good idea but I have reservations. I find it almost impossible with the numbers I teach to really do it justice as I would like to."

4. *Coming on to the children's reading in Gaelic —*

(a) *Do they read much more/or some read more/or much the same as before?*

Table 4(a)

Much more	Some read more	Same	N/A
14	23	8	8

(b) *Do they read Gaelic more fluently/or less fluently/or the same as before?*

Table 4(b)

More fluently	Same	Less fluently	N/A
33	12	—	8

(c) *In reading Gaelic do they make more mistakes/or fewer mistakes/or the same as before?*

Table 4(c)

More mistakes	Same	Fewer mistakes	N/A
1	19	24	9

These tables show that the project has had a significant effect on children's reading in Gaelic. 70% of teachers stated that the children read more, 63% said that the children read more fluently and 46% said that the children make fewer mistakes than before.

Comments — "All of them read a lot more than they used to but some of read a lot more than others do. I think they make fewer (mistakes) because we have so much more practice. We read Gaelic every day."

— "I do more reading to the children. They read what they themselves write, more fluently. Anxious to read what their classmates have written."

— "I think they tend to read more in Gaelic and I think they're more fluent. They're more used to the words. I read it straight through and that makes them more familiar with the words and that makes them inclined to make less mistakes."

5. *Now their reading in English —*
   (a) *Do they read English more fluently/or less fluently/or the same as before?*

Table 5(a)

More fluently	Less fluently	Same	N/A
6	—	43	4

(b) *In reading English do they make more mistakes/fewer mistakes/or the same as before?*

Table 5(b)

More mistakes	Fewer mistakes	Same	N/A
1	2	46	4

6. *Do they spend less time reading English now/or more time/or much the same?*

Table 6

Less time	More time	Same	N/A
5	14	27	7

These data show that the children's progress in the project has not been at the expense of their work in English. A number of teachers felt that more time is spent on English reading than in previous years: this is likely to be the result of more imaginative use of children's fiction in primary school. Six teachers noted that the children are more fluent than before in their reading of English.

Comments — "I think they probably spend more time reading now. Children's novels and so on. The new children's books they find more interesting."
— "I think they spend more time reading English now because they get a supply of very good books from the library."
— "I think on balance they probably read more in English as well as in Gaelic. The reading has developed quite a lot." quite a lot."

7. *Now their writing in Gaelic —*
    (a) Do they write much more than before/more/or do some write more/or the same as before?

Table 7(a)

Much more	More	Some write more	Same	Less	N/A
4	30	12	1	—	6

  (b) *Do they write Gaelic more fluently/or less fluently/or the same as before?*

Table 7(b)

More fluently	Same	Less	N/A
34	9	—	10

(c) *In writing Gaelic do they make more mistakes/or fewer mistakes/or the same as before?*

Table 7(c)

More mistakes	Same	Fewer	N/A
8	8	26	11

The amount and quality of children's writing in Gaelic has increased significantly during the time of the project. Prior to the project, children's writing in Gaelic tended to be developed even less than their reading. While 70% of teachers (Table 4(a)) stated that Gaelic reading has increased, Table 7(a) shows that 87% of teachers said that children's writing in Gaelic has increased.

Comments — "The majority write much more than before, because we use it as an integral part of the project. We record many of our feelings in Gaelic. All our drama is in Gaelic, so in fact we write much more."

— "Well, original work, there's more of that . . . They do have more to say, to write."

— "I have a P7 at the moment who are writing things that I would never have seen myself teaching before in Gaelic."

— "They're better at making up their own writing now that they were before."

8. *In their writing in English —*
    (a) *Do they write much more than before/or some write more/or the same as before?*

Table 8(a)

Much more	Some write more	Same	Less	N/A
6	12	29	2	4

(b) *Do they write English more fluently/or less fluently/or the same as before?*

Table 8(b)

More fluently	Same	Less	N/A
10	34	2	7

(c) *In writing English do they make more mistakes/or fewer mistakes/or the same as before?*

Table 8(c)

More mistakes	Same	Less	N/A
3	41	5	4

Most of the teachers felt that the children's writing in English was on a par with what it had been in previous years. A number of teachers felt that the standards here had improved: a few felt they had been lowered.

Comments — "It hasn't affected their English at all."

— "I don't know that the project has made much difference to their written English because new attitudes had developed towards English writing before the project started."

— "I don't think it has altered. It certainly hasn't suffered, but I can't say that it's better."

— "More mistakes, but then again they are writing more."

9. *Now the children's speaking Gaelic —*

(a) *When the children want to speak to you or ask a question, do they use Gaelic more than they did before?*
    (Yes, much more/Yes, a little more/No/or difficult to say).

Table 9(a)

Much more	A little more	Same	Less	Difficult to say	N/A
8	15	17	—	5	8

(b) *Do they tend to speak to each other in Gaelic in the classroom, more than was the case before?*
    (Yes, much/Yes, a little more/No/or difficult to say).

Table 9(b)

Much more	A little more	Same	Less	Difficult to say	N/A
7	8	25	1	6	6

(c) *Do you speak to them more in Gaelic in the classroom than you might have done before?*
(Much more/a little more/the same as before).

Table 9(c)

Much more	More	A little more	Same	Less	N/A
4	20	12	10	1	6

These three tables show an interesting pattern in that the most significant increase reported in the use of spoken Gaelic in the classroom is that of teacher to child (67%), the next most significant increase is that of child to teacher (43%), while the increase between child and child is 28%.

Comments — "They use it more than they did before, especially the non-Gaelic speakers. They now try to speak in Gaelic."
— "Yes much more. Their approach within the classroom is quite different really. They ask in Gaelic and tell me a story in Gaelic a lot more than previously."
— "Some of them used to talk to each other in Gaelic anyway."
— "I had begun to speak in Gaelic to them before the project."
— "I suppose with more Gaelic books and using the medium of Gaelic more, I'm bound to use more."
— "The majority tend to ask questions in English yet."

10. *Now their use of Gaelic in the playground —*
Do they use it more often than before/no difference?

Table 10

More	Same	Less	N/A
3	37	7	6

Comments — "No difference as far as I could see."
— "No difference. Actually I would say there is less (Gaelic)."
— "We have more incomers now so it's difficult to gauge if they're using more Gaelic."

— "We hear them speak English in the playground, I'm afraid."

11. *The children's interest in Gaelic —*
    Are they more interested or less interested in Gaelic than before?
    Table 11

More interested	Same	Less	N/A
36	5	4	8

Comments — "I find them asking for Gaelic stories, Gaelic reading. They had never done this before."
— "They don't feel any difference — Gaelic or English. They don't react and say, 'Let's have it in English'."
— "In the classroom anyway they show more interest in reading Gaelic and doing things in Gaelic than they did in the past."
— "More. Because they get such a variety of things, subjects catered for. When we went on our outings and bus trips we spoke in Gaelic."

12. *Has the work of the project affected what the children learn about?*
    Table 12

Yes	No	N/A
41	3	9

Comments — "Because we've been going out a lot more they're more aware of their own environment."
— "Yes, because a much wider field has been opened for us to work in."
— "Yes, for they are very interested in their own environment, in ourselves, in what they see and hear. No hesitation in talking about everything. They take note of the birds, when they came and when they go. Croft work too."
— "It brought the home into what they do in school."

13. *Would you say that your relationship with the children is different in any way as a result of your involvement with the project?*

Table 13

Yes	No	Difficult to say	N/A
19	30	2	2

Comments — "No, I don't think so. I feel I have a fairly good relationship with them."
— "Well, I wouldn't think so, because I was speaking Gaelic to them from the very first time I came here."
— "I think we speak more to each other. It isn't just all teaching."
— "Going out has made it more relaxed than being in the classroom all the time."
— "What I can say is that it is very different to the relationship one had with pupils 20 years ago."

14. *The project has been involved in producing Gaelic books —*
    (a) *Have you found the books useful?*
    (b) *Do the children find them enjoyable?*
Fifty out of the 53 teachers said that they had found the books useful and that the children had found them enjoyable.

Comments — "Yes, they've all been very useful one way or another."
— "They're so much more attractive than the old types of Gaelic books."
— "Some of them are quite useful."
— "Yes, more so than the old mundane sort of books they used to get in Gaelic."

(c) *Which books have the children liked best?*
Table 14 lists the books mentioned by teachers.

Table 14

Title	no of re-sponses
"Spàgan" series (12 titles)	37
"MacCurraich" books (2 titles)	14
"Uilleam Bàn agus an Iolaire"	12
"Blàir Mhór an t-Saoghail" series (4 titles)	6
Stick-on books (8 titles)	5
"Cliath" books for P1-3 (3 titles)	3
"Leagsaidh Luchag"	3
"Tùs Leughaidh" series (8 titles)	2
"Tugainn Cuairt"	1

(d) *Have you any criticism of (i) the pictures; (ii) the choice of words; (iii) contents?*

From the responses to these questions it is clear that almost all the teachers are very satisfied with the books which have been produced. The pictures were highly regarded. One teacher's comment, "No criticism whatsoever, because it works" seems to typify the general response. There was virtually no criticism of the content of books. A few teachers mentioned that words used were sometimes a little difficult; that some of the words were regional (eg Lewis words) and that the spelling was sometimes rather anglicised.

15. *The non-Gaelic speaking children —*
   (a) *To what extent do these children join in the Gaelic work going on, or do they do something else at that time?*

Table 15(a)

Join in	Do something else	N/A
44	6	3

(b) *Are they now learning to speak more Gaelic than in previous years?*

Table 15(c)

Yes	No	N/A
26	11	16

Teachers in project schools generally seek to involve non-Gaelic speaking children as fully as possible in the work of the project and in half the classrooms in the project these children are learning to speak Gaelic more than in previous years.

Comments — (a) "They join in with everything and what they can't write in Gaelic they write in English."

(b) "Well, that I can't say because I haven't had any non-Gaelic speaking children before."

— (a) "They join in with everybody else."

(b) "Not really. But I've always considered them Gaelic speaking. Whether they're Gaelic speaking or not they seem to join in."

— (a) "They usually do something else."

(b) "No."

— (a) "They are fully involved in the work that the Gaelic-speaking children do."

(b) "O, yes. Much more."

— (a) "They are encouraged to work in with the other children. At no time do I allow them to do anything else."

(b) "Yes, the non-Gaelic speaking children have bene-fited from the project, I would say, more than fluent Gaelic speakers, in that I have now one or two children who are now becoming fluent speakers who hitherto were non-Gaelic speakers."

— (a) "Well I try to take them along with the Gaelic speakers as much as possible, and the only thing is — What I would like really is more material for these children."

16. *Now parents' reaction to the project — Would you say they are interested/not interested/varied in interest/or difficult to say?*

Table 16

Interested	Not interested	Varied interest	Difficult to say
16	3	17	9

Comments — "Difficult to say because I haven't seen them together as a group."

— "Very interested in any activities we're doing in the school and certainly they were very interested in this, and they're very keen that their own children speak Gaelic and they themselves try to speak more to them than they did in the past."

— "I don't come into contact with many of the parents."

— "The parents I've spoken to have been in favour."

— "You get quite a lot of support from the parents, and at each parent meeting we've had for the last 2-3 years they have shown quite a lot of interest and indeed were quite impressed with some of it."

— "Not interested. I haven't seen or heard any comment from them."

17. (a) *What do you like about the project?*

Table 17

Aspects mentioned	No of Teachers
— the local environment as a learning resource	18
— the back-up and support provided by the team	9
— the variety of themes offered	9
— the books and other resources provided	6
— the increased interest in Gaelic and in the children's skills in the language	6
— the teachers' group meetings	6
— the approach recommended by the project	3

— that it makes children more observant   2
— the project's "largeness"   1
— the project's informality   1
— the project's "new ideas"   1

Comments — "I like the variety, because it was a bit tedious doing the same exercise book year after year."
— "I like meeting the other teachers and hearing all the grand things that they're doing."
— "The children learning to speak in their native tongue, for
— a start."
— "I like the way that we were able to push the wall of the classroom down and go into the environment so much. It's a lot wider, the learning we do. I like the largeness of it."

(b) *What changes would you suggest?*

The changes suggested by teachers in reply to question 17b were that the individual teacher should now be given more autonomy (12); that the keeping of a diary should be discontinued (3); that there should be less emphasis on writing and more on speaking and reading (4); that there should be fewer meetings (1); fewer visits to schools by team members (1); more consultation with teachers (1); that Gaelic speaking children entering school should receive no English on Primary 1 and 2 (1); that the project should "slow down" (1); and that there should be "a complete rethink" (1) — the last-mentioned being a teacher who liked "nothing" about the project. Twenty-seven teachers stated they they would like the project to continue as it is with no changes.

18. *Have you any general comments to add?*

Ten teachers said they had enjoyed the project and did not elaborate, while 18 teachers had no general comments to make. The difficulties caused by the increasing numbers of English-speaking children in schools were mentioned by 9 teachers, and 6 teachers stated that the co-operation of parents should be sought. Other comments made by one or two teachers included appreciation of the Gaelic radio programmes for schools and the need for Gaelic programmes on TV; that the project should be extended to all schools; that the "poorer ones" should be excluded from the project; that the project was very time-consuming, or expected too much of the children, or applied too much pressure upon teachers, or was too difficult to organise.

Discussion

The data from the teachers' interviews highlight how most teachers believe that the children have gained in a number of ways as a result of the work of the project. Most teachers feel that the children read more Gaelic and do so more fluently and with fewer mistakes. The children's writing of Gaelic has similarly benefited in that most teachers state that the children write more Gaelic and do so more fluently and with fewer mistakes. The project is also seen as having a significant effect on how Gaelic is spoken in the classroom — the strongest effect being on the teacher's use of Gaelic in speaking to the children. The project has had more effect on peer-group use of Gaelic in the classroom than in the playground, and it is worthy of note that most teachers see a positive change in the children's attitude towards Gaelic.

While such gains have been observed by the teachers in the children's use of Gaelic, it is interesting to note that virtually all the teachers feel that the children's standard of reading and writing in English has not been affected adversely during the time of the project. In fact, 14 teachers stated that children now spend more time reading English than they did in previous years, and 18 teachers feel that they now write more in English than they did before. A number of factors could have caused this increase, including the extensive English language arts in-service work that has gone on in the Western Isles in parallel with the project, and also the fact that the work of the project, while ostensibly concerned with Gaelic, is likely to have had a positive effect on other parts of the primary curriculum, including English.

The teachers' observations on the non-Gaelic speaking children is of interest. In most of the classrooms these children join in with the Gaelic speaking children rather than being involved in some other part of the curriculum. This requires considerable organisation and effort and the need was expressed for more materials suitable for young learners. Half the teachers felt that these children are learning to speak more Gaelic than in previous years. Previously, of course, it was not unusual for non-Gaelic speaking children to learn some Gaelic while attending these schools.

There is much enthusiasm among the teachers for the new Gaelic books, which have come into the schools as a result of the project. This is not surprising when the baseline was so low in terms of number and quality before the project began. Teachers frequently express the wish to see many more Gaelic books, especially for infants and top primary pupils. There is little doubt that the "Spàgan" books were the ones which made the most impact, both with teachers and children. As one teacher said, "Spàgan is Top of the Pops".

Parents have seen more of the project's work through the new books than through any other part. There is considerable variation between schools in the extent to which parents have the opportunity to see the work going on in the schools, including that of the project. There is every indication that parents have been interested in the work of the project whenever it has been explained to them as an integral part of the curriculum.

Most teachers feel that the work of the project has had an effect on what the children learn, in that it has utilized the child's local language, culture and environment as learning resources. This also entailed a new mode of learning in that it necessitated more practical work, more learning outside the classroom setting and more shared discovery by teacher and pupil.

All this has meant that a fair number of teachers recognise that being involved in the project in this way has given rise to a new kind of relationship between themselves and the children — one which tends to be more informal with mutual involvement in the learning process. Teachers and children generally have closer relationships nowadays than in the past. Some project teachers are aware of an even more informal atmosphere when they are utilising the methods and approach of the project.

It is interesting to note that most teachers enjoyed being in the project. Most of them had felt that it was a good idea from the start and even more of them think so now. The methods and content of the project, as well as its organisation, won the approval of the majority of the teachers involved. A number of them now wish to be given more autonomy in developing the work further. There is every indication that most teachers improved the quality and range of their teaching as a result of their involvement in the project. Such improvement is essential to the aims of the project, for, as Stenhouse wrote, "there can be no educational development without teacher development . . ." (Stenhouse)[9]

PART TWO: A Radio Documentary

Transcript (translated) of a 45-minute Gaelic programme: "The Project: A survey of the work of the Bilingual Education Project in the Western Isles", broadcast on BBC Radio Scotland, VHF, on 26 January 1978.

Notes:

1. Editorial control of this programme was exercised by the BBC in the normal way: while the producer discussed the form and content of the programme with the project team, he was entirely responsible for the final programme.
2. The programme as broadcast consisted of responses to interviewer's questions which were edited out; there are no prepared statements in the programme.
3. Speakers, other than Donald Cameron who produced and presented the programme, in order of appearance:

    Dr Finlay MacLeod, Primary Adviser, Comhairle nan Eilean
    John A Smith, Chairman, Consultative Committee
    John Murray, director, Bilingual Education Project
    Christina Murray, Assistant Head Teacher, Shawbost Primary School, Lewis
    Christina Smith, Assistant Teacher, Kildonan Primary School, South Uist
    Anna Morrison, Assistant Teacher, Lionel Primary School, Lewis
    Jean Stewart, Head Teacher, Kallin School, North Uist
    Greta MacKenzie, Head Teacher, Knockiandue School, Lewis
    Effie MacQuarrie, Assistant Head Teacher, Paible (Bayhead) Primary School, North Uist
    Catherine Morrison, Research Assistant, Bilingual Education Project
    Annie MacDonald, Research Assistant, Bilingual Education Project
    Lachlan Dick, Gaelic Adviser, Comhairle nan Eilean
    Annie MacDonald, Fieldworker, Community Education Project
    Jo MacDonald, BBC Schools Department, Producer
    Rev J M M MacArthur, Chairman, Education Committee, Comhairle nan Eilean.

Finlay MacLeod:

When any aspect of education has been neglected, there are various ways of trying to renew and reinvigorate it. In my opinion, the most interesting way is to set up a project. A project is a means of encouraging, of directing attention in such a way as to make people talk about that part of education, be it bilingualism or the environment or anything like that. And then, little by little, people come to see that as an integral part of education in general, and become aware that staff should be engaged to work in that area, that money should be spent in it.

Presenter:
Finlay MacLeod, Primary Adviser in the Western Isles, answering
what is, perhaps, the principal question in the minds of people about
the Bilingual Education Project: why is the work in a project structure?

Finlay MacLeod was also involved in the preliminary stages of
formation of the project.

Finlay MacLeod:
In education all over the world, one of the new things you see — say,
in the last decade or so — is that a number of bilingual programmes
have appeared, in almost every country in the world. For example, in
America a Bilingual Education Act was passed in 1968 and since then
about 300 programmes have been established in the States. Everybody knows that the teaching of a second and third language in
secondary school has been going on for a long time, but now that has
been developed into bilingual education and instead of being a
question — a problem, as it were — now it is something which attracts
a lot of attention all over the world.

The Director of Education we had here two years before Comhairle
nan Eilean was established — that was Bob Inglis — arranged that an
adviser should be appointed to look after Gaelic and Primary education in the islands and I was appointed to that post. In these days,
excellent work was being done in schools with regard to Gaelic
although teachers were working as independent individuals. There
had been advisers before then: Inverness County Council had done
much to refresh things in the southern islands, there was the work
done by Dr MacLean and Murdo MacLeod and so on. But I realised
that no single person would be able to set up and develop the kind of
bilingual education that was required when the Western Isles Islands
Area was created.

I was aware of the work being undertaken by the Schools Council in
England and Wales with regard to bilingual education, especially in
Wales: at that time, I think, they had five projects in progress.
Scotland is not within the area of the Schools Council, so the need for
this kind of education in the Western Isles had to be put to the Scottish
Education Department. In various ways that was done — at conferences such as "Interskola" and so on — and by means of a committee
concerned with Gaelic textbooks we made a case to the SED for such a
scheme to be established: this was before Comhairle nan Eilean was
begun. There was a Steering Committee in the Islands at that time but
they did not consider Gaelic or the place of Gaelic. The SED told us
they were willing to consider the proposals and a group of us went to

Edinburgh. The proposals were accepted and the Department agreed
to allocate funds. The Director of Education in the Western Isles was
informed and he advised us to go ahead, that the Authority would
investigate the possibility of offering joint financial support.

From the time we submitted the proposals to the SED, the most
surprising thing was the speed with which the Department moved and
how interested they were in the project — as they have remained until
now.

John A Smith:

The SED came to Jordanhill College because, according to regula-
tions, they cannot pay money directly to a Council for a purpose such
as this — only to a college or university.

This work had already begun in various ways. I remember the
Research Council in Edinburgh, which worked for years, issuing
publications and studying the development of Gaelic in education.
After this beginning, Inverness County Council began to give greater
assistance to Gaelic and Murdo MacLeod was the first Gaelic Adviser
in Scotland. Other committees were looking at the progress of Gaelic
matters. In this way, all these efforts came together with the opportunity offered by the project to take a bold step forward in the teaching
of Gaelic.

Finlay MacLeod:

A director was found, John Murray, and gradually, accommodation
was obtained in Stornoway, and in the early days of Comhairle nan
Eilean, the project was established and got under way in the schools.

Presenter:

As well as Finlay MacLeod, you heard John A Smith, who was
Vice-Principal of Jordanhill College at the time, in 1975.

John Murray:

The schools are the heart of the project. It is in the schools you see
whether things are going to work or not.

Shawbost School
(Christina Murray with class)

C Murray: There was a lot of snow this week. Did you enjoy it?
Pupils: (in chorus) Yes.
C Murray: And where is it now?
Pupils: It went away, it's gone . . etc.
C Murray: Did the rain wash it all away?
Pupils: Yes.
C Murray: What colour was the snow?

Pupils: White.

C Murray: Do you remember that we made up our own poem about colours, the beautiful colours in the room and the colours we saw when we were out for a walk?

Pupils: (throughout) — Yes — we remember . . . etc.

C Murray: Will you say the poem for us, John Norman?

John Norman: Yes, I'll say it.

One, two, three, butter is yellow
Four, five, six, grass is green
Seven, eight, nine, Carol's bag is brown
Ten, eleven, twelve, isn't purple beautiful?

Christina Murray:

This is our third year in the project and in this room the children are aged from 5 to 7 years. The reading material used is material concerning their own lives, their own families and homes, what happens in their homes, what they themselves do at home, their own games and activities outside, and anything else of that kind that they bring up. But talking comes first, getting them to talk first about anything that is of interest to them. We give them books, and we discuss things we come across in books. They learn single words first, then they go on to little stories which they themselves make up about these things we find in books.

When we go out, we try to go to places where the children, firstly, will be able to run about and play. Then they look for things which they take back to the room and we make charts and other things which are put on the walls. They talk about these. Usually they want to take these things home with them so that their parents will see them.

There are twenty-one pupils here. Only four of them do not come from Gaelic homes, but they are making good progress with learning it. One boy, Norman, is just as good at reading Gaelic as the rest. He wasn't willing to speak Gaelic at first, but today he talks it outside and he can read it well and write some as well. The others are making progress too. Norman tells me that his mother does not have good Gaelic and that he himself is teaching her Gaelic!

Kildonan School
Christina Smith:

This is our third year in the project and the children in this room are the first three classes.

I began to take them out for walks, and they were very interested in taking note of everything they saw. When we came back we would talk further about what had been seen and then they drew pictures of

55

whatever had attracted them most. Later we began to do a little writing about it. I would put words on the blackboard for them to use in their own books. Usually the drawings they did would be put up on the wall and we wrote beneath them. I saw that this brought them on very much in reading and also in writing. Also, they themselves enjoyed discussing these things — things which they saw round about them.

I notice now that when they talk, they show a good knowledge of what they are talking about. And, if one person were to say today, "I saw a heron," or whatever it might be, the others will try to see it that evening so that they can talk about it tomorrow and so that they will have something to tell that the first person did not.

Just now I am doing the theme "Snow". With the first class, I gave them the word *snow*. From that we got *snowman, I made a snowman, we made a snowman* . . . The children recognise these words and they will substitute *mammy*, or *daddy* for *I*. In this way they are learning all the time.

Each week we discuss the programmes (ie BBC Schools Gaelic Series *Culaidh Mhiogais*), we make drawings about them — and do some writing too. We also learn some of the poems and some of the songs that the children like.

Kildonan School
Children P1-3:
(Children singing a lively song from the programme "Uisge" in the series *Culaidh Mhiogais*.)

Kildonan School
Christina Smith:
Oh, I have learned many things since the project began. For instance, I did not know much about birds, but now I recognise many more.

Usually, if I see at teachers' meetings some school is trying something different, I will try that and if I like it, I will go ahead. But if I do not, I leave it at that.

Presenter:
A description there of some of what is going on in two schools, with the youngest pupils. You heard Christina Murray from Shawbost School in Lewis and Christina Smith from Kildonan School, South Uist.

Now, some of the work being done in schools by children in the middle range of primary. First, Anna Morrison from Lionel School in Lewis and then Jean Stewart from Kallin School, in North Uist.

Lionel School
Anna Morrison:

This is my second year in the project and in each year I've had primary 4 and 5.

The book I am using just now, "The Boy with the Bronze Axe", I read to them in English, but much of the discussion we have about the book is in Gaelic, and it's the same in writing — we do writing in English and in Gaelic about the contents of the book. We are enjoying it very much and I think we are succeeding in linking it with the children's own background. We went especially to the Eoropie temple. There were archaeologists there at the time who showed us some of the things in the temple and told us how these things were used in the distant past. As well as that, the children asked at home about the history of this place and we discovered information in that way.

I think the skills are taught as they always were, but, perhaps we are using different ways of doing so. The work is different and it means that I have to use different methods, but — well, there's no shortage of work anyway!

Kallin School
Jean Stewart:

We found the book "The Boy with the Bronze Axe" a simple, easy book which gave the children a good description of the homes and way of life of people of that period.

At the beginning of autumn, we listened to the programme about Udal in the *Co Iad?* series and although this went back a long long way in time, the site itself was near to us, and the children enjoyed that. From that we proceeded to writing about it, and indeed they let their imagination soar in doing this. We linked the book with Udal and with other places in North Uist. We intend to go to Cliatraval to see the stone dwellings there and the day we go there we will carry out a lot of measurement and other preparation for mapwork.

English, Gaelic, painting, writing, history, geography, arithmetic — everything you can think of is included in these lessons. There is a good deal of additional work involved but I see that we are covering much more ground.

Presenter:

Now, another two schools and this time the older pupils. First Greta MacKenzie in Knockiandue School and then Effie MacQuarrie in Paible School in North Uist.

So that you will understand what is happening in the following

57

classroom recording: Greta has been discussing with the children the story of the book "Hill's End" which they have been reading. It is set in Australia.

Knockiandue School
(Greta MacKenzie with Class)

Greta MacKenzie: When they came upon the cave paintings, they went further and further into the cave. They didn't expect to discover that place, they just happened to find it. They looked at the paintings. Time passed, and while they were in the cave — what happened, Donald?

Donald: Thunder and lightning began and water poured into the cave and they had to go up on to ledges.

Greta MacKenzie: We composed a poem about that storm. Will you read it, Hector?

Hector: Lightning
    thunder
    rain pouring down
    hailstones like your fist
    dark sky
    The wind blowing, blowing, BLOWING

    We are in the cave
    a dark cavern,
    cold, lonely and eerie
    rainwater in rivulets
    thunder beating
    lightning flashing
    water rising, rising, RISING

    we will be drowned
    the girls are crying
    Miss Godwin has deserted us
    we cannot be saved
    my heart leaping
    my heart boiling
    my feet frozen
    I am shivering
    with fear
    FEAR OF MY LIFE.

Greta MacKenzie:

Well, I began in the project when the school opened in August, and the children I have are from 8 to 11 years old — that is P4, 5, 6, 7. In my opinion we got on very well in the first term because of the assistance given to us by the project team in Stornoway.

We received notes on the book we were reading and that helped us to get off to a good start. Once we got started on that book (ie "Hill's End") the thing took off — I would almost say, by itself.

In English, we did some of the history and geography of Australia. In Gaelic, the children were comparing themselves and the way of life here with the way the children in a place like Hill's End lived. When we discussed the way of life of these children in Australia, we also built up a picture of our way of life. Just as in Hill's End they had a wood mill, we have here a seaweed factory. We studied the work being done there, how many people are employed there, how much this benefits the village — that most men from Keose and several from Laxay earn their living there.

On a good day we would go out for a walk, taking the camera with us. At first, I set about getting the children to talk freely. I found at first that it was difficult for the children to do this — to discuss. From morning till dusk — you could say — we talk in both languages and work in both languages. Because of this, their ability to speak is advancing well, they are more ready to talk to myself in Gaelic, for instance, when they ask me for something. And when I want to say anything to them in class, I say it in Gaelic instead of English. Never again will I say, "Please close the door!" (ie in English).

Paible School
Effie MacQuarrie:

It's over a year now since I became involved in the work of the project. I teach classes 5 to 7.

We read an English book called "Sula" by Lavinia Derwent. Sula was an island, like this place itself with a little village, a port, children going to school and so on. From this book we did reading and writing in both English and Gaelic. The children drew a picture of the place described in the book and they constructed a model showing all the buildings in the village in Sula. Then they made a plan based on the model. They wrote about the work as it progressed in Gaelic and in English. From there we went on to make a plan of our classroom and then of the school. At last we went to Caolas — a village near the school. We measured — in paces — the houses, the distances between them and the shore, the fences and so on. When we had all the measurements we made a model of Caolas from these measurements, then we drew a plan from the model. We got a large-scale map of the area and we saw how similar it was to the map we ourselves had made.

We got the history of Caolas from Shonny Dhodaidh. We investigated the type of soil at Caolas. We studied crofting. We went to the cattle sale, following the Caolas cattle from the time they left Caolas until they went aboard the ship at Lochmaddy.

Usually, we do the project work in the afternoons. The mornings we spend on mathematics and reading and writing. But I think it is obvious that every subject is included in the work of the project — number work, literacy, history, geography, art, handwork and so on.

John Murray:

The schools are the heart of the project. It is in the schools you see whether things are going to work or not.

Presenter:

From the schools, then, to the project team itself: John Murray — the director — Catherine Morrison and Annie MacDonald.

John Murray:

There are 20 schools, from Ness in Lewis to Eoligarry in Barra in the project and these were chosen for various reasons. One reason is that a team of three can only do so much work in a day or in a year, but more important, we had in mind the need to have a distribution of schools throughout the islands and the need for different sizes of school to be involved. Also, we looked at the strength of Gaelic in the neighbourhood of the school, because the project was set up for the benefit of bilingual children in the first place.

There were plenty of problems at first, as there are with anything new which is being established, One of the problems, because we were going to work in islands, was the way that the team should operate. We chose to split the team, so that Annie would work in Uist and Catherine in Lewis — and I myself am based in Lewis. And although that caused difficulties at first, since it split the team and it was not easy for us to get together as often as we should like to, I think it worked out well eventually, because it brings the project closer to the schools and that is what we want to do. There were other problems. At the beginning, we faced crucial questions about the way in which we should work, how we should become engaged in schools, what part teachers should play in the project, how we should work educationally — what kind of education, what kind of teaching. These are important questions, and we spent long weeks — the team by itself and with others, consulting others, and I think we evolved a very good way of working and that we chose an area of schooling which is very suitable for bilingual education.

Catherine Morrison:

I started in the project when it began, in September 1975. We in the project team provide guidance for teachers, we research educational methods and consider what approaches we are going to try out to achieve the kind of bilingual education we are aiming at in our schools.

The teachers themselves participate to a great extent in planning and in the choice of ways to be used. We hold meetings of teachers very frequently. These meetings are a vitally important part of the work of the project. They bring the teachers together, they enable them to meet and to discuss. Teachers talk about the work they are doing, they tell each other how it was done, they listen and learn from one another, they discuss their work and they discuss education in general.

Annie MacDonald:

I attend ten schools between North Uist, South Uist, Eriskay and Barra. My work is to direct the activities of the project in these schools.

The situation of every school is different, but the teachers make use of their own environment in school, first to stimulate talk among the children, and to teach drawing, reading and writing. Then, as the children grow older, the environment is used for teaching geography, history and natural science, all these being interlinked. There is a steady progress to learning about other places, as you heard when "Boy with the Bronze Axe" and "Hill's End" were spoken of.

John Murray:

We are proceeding in various ways to involve parents in the work of the school. It was not usual for Gaelic parents — nor indeed for parents in Scotland as a whole — to participate in the work of the school. One of the ways we use is that we have held meetings — in eight of the twenty schools — especially to explain to parents what our purpose is in the project, what sort of education we are talking about and what this means for their children. Often at meetings — and this is true of any meeting here — it is easier for strangers who have come into the Gaelic area to speak out than it is for the Gaels themselves. Perhaps this has something to do with education, but it does seem to be more difficult for a Gael to speak out than for a non-Gael and that is one of the very important questions which has to be considered by us.

It is not possible for the project team to carry out all the work that requires to be done and we have to work together with other agencies and individuals. We work daily with some, such as officials of Comhairle nan Eilean, especially those in the Education Department.

Lachlan Dick: (Gaelic Adviser)

With regard to making comparison between the schools within the project and those that are not, it is certainly clear that the project influences the kind of work that goes on in the schools in which it is involved. I think we must remember, however, that it is not possible in a year or two to alleviate the results of more than one hundred years of neglect.

I think the most remarkable thing I see is the way in which project schools approach Gaelic. No longer do they look upon it as a subject, but as a teaching medium and thus they handle various subjects through the medium of Gaelic. Now I know there are schools outwith the project which do the same and so the thing cannot be set down in black and white terms.

John Murray:

We are also daily in discussion and co-operation with the project team of the Community Education Project.

Annie Macdonald: (Community Education Project)

We work very closely sometimes with the Bilingual Project. If you look at it this way: the Bilingual Project works inside the school and sometimes goes out into the neighbourhood, and on the other hand the Community Education Project works in the neighbourhood and sometimes goes into the schools, in the same sort of pattern.

The children attend school from 9 to 4 o'clock. The rest of the time, they are members of some community and thus anything that is going on in the community affects these children. In a few years these children will not be in school, they will be out in the community, and as our project spreads out across the islands, I think the co-operation between the two projects will spread through the islands also.

John Murray:

Also, there are groups with whom we work often — for example, the Gaelic Department of the Schools Broadcasting Department of BBC Scotland.

Jo MacDonald: (Producer, BBC Schools)

The project and the Schools Department of the BBC work together in various ways, and this has been going on almost since the project first began, and since we first began. We co-operate in the choice of subjects for programmes, ensuring that we are not pulling in different directions, that we go in the same general direction, We get a lot of support from the team in helping teachers to make the best use of our programmes in schools. We meet the project team — I do — quite often in Uist and in Stornoway, to discuss what we are doing, whether we are doing it in the best way. Also, as producer, I work with a committee and the project is represented on that committee which plans our programmes about a year and a half in advance.

John Murray:
There are others with whom we do not co-operate on a daily or regular basis, but we work together with them for a specific purpose — for example, we and An Comunn Gaidhealach and the Highlands and Islands Development Board worked together to produce six books last year, and that has now been advanced a step. We went further. Comhairle nan Eilean took an active interest and there is now a new publishing company called *Acair* for the purpose of publishing general educational books in Gaelic.

Still in this group of those who work with us for specific reasons, Stirling University is working with us to make video-cassettes on themes related to the environment — geography, knowledge of birds, of shores and things of that kind. We are well ahead with this and we hope these will be published sometime this year.

We also co-operate with Jordanhill College, which sends up to the islands each year some of their Gaelic-speaking students who are in the last year of their training. These spend their time in project schools and in that way they become familiar with the way of teaching which we recommend to schools and which schools are using.

Annie MacDonald:
Here in Uist, Cinema Sgire has begun and we see that use can be made of the equipment that project offers. This year we have organised with Cinema Sgire that they should follow the work which is going on in one school on a historical theme connected with the place. As well as that they are useful to us for teachers' meetings and for in-service training of teachers and it shows the general public what is going on in education just now.

John Murray:
We write and exchange information with other projects in Britain, in Europe, across the Atlantic and in other places worldwide, for we believe it is our duty to tell the world about the islands and at the same time to get information from across the world into the islands and to feed that into the schools.

Presenter:
In the remainder of this part of the programme, you will hear the Rev Jack MacArthur, chairman of the Education Committee of Comhairle

nan Eilean, as well as Finlay MacLeod and John A Smith whom you heard at the beginning, talking about the project.

Rev J MacArthur:

We must always remember that it is a project, that other work must be going ahead all the time in all the schools, in secondary and primary schools. The project is seen by us as something especially useful to improve the situation which existed before and for giving expression to opinions as to what we ought to be doing in the years ahead. It is going to be most helpful in spreading out to all the schools new ways of teaching, new books and publications, so that parents and children and the whole population will see the use of the two languages instead of one in a different light.

The project, viewed in one way, is working by itself as something separate. It has the independence necessary to introduce new ideas, to try new things in schools, but at the same time, the team has to work along with our own officials.

Finlay MacLeod:

To some extent the project is engaged in working with adults. It is with teachers in the first instance that the project works. Through talk, through discussion, through bringing resources to them — it is with attitudes of adults and what value is given to the subject that one is concerned. To the children, some of the ways in which the project is put to work in the schools are merely another part of school work.

John A Smith:

At present I am the Chairman of the Consultative Committee whose role is to monitor the project. We hope that eventually the project will be an undertaking that lasts, over the Gaelic areas as a whole.

Rev J MacArthur

There is a lot going for the islands just now. I don't think the people understand how much is happening and how useful this is going to be in the years ahead. As far as Gaelic is concerned, I think the project is the most effective development that has come, because we are getting through to children, teachers and parents. Once they understand what underlies the project, what we are trying to achieve by means of the project, I think it will be seen as the most advantageous thing to happen as far as language is concerned in the islands in the lifetime of anyone today.

Presenter:

But what is yet to come in the project? The last words to the Rev Jack

MacArthur and Finlay MacLeod. But first we'll return to John Murray.

John Murray:
The principal tasks facing us in the second part of the project from 1978 on are first to strengthen what we have gained up to this stage in the schools. By that I mean more books, preparation of more materials which suit the way of teaching which we recommend — and we have established methods of ensuring this, that work will come from the teachers themselves and return to themselves. The second — and major — task is to go into all the schools in the Western Isles, if we are able. Just now I don't know if that is possible, but I hope it will be. And since there are only three in the team and it is utterly beyond the capabilities of the three of us to do this, another one member will be coming into the project team.

Rev J MacArthur:
The Council is allocating much more money to the project for the three years to come than it gave in the three years past. That shows, in my opinion, that the Council is fully satisfied with the work done by the project up to present — and that the Council realises it is getting quite a lot out of the project with regard to the work going on in schools! Not only are we content with what has been done — we see the necessity for us to carry forward what the project has begun. For too long people thought Gaelic did not have the same status as English. We say it has, it ought by rights to have, and that it will have in the future. It is not only language we are dealing with — we are concerned with the culture and the history of the islands.

John Murray:
We could not tackle everything. It is only two years and a few weeks ago that we went into schools and there is much still to be done. There are many things which we regret not having worked at sufficiently so far, and that will be so for years yet. This is a huge task which will take a long time.

We must also in the second phase of the project consider what will confront these children when they go to secondary school. The Education Department in the islands and, in my opinion, the Scottish Education Department must take responsibility to ensure that every talent and every capability which children in the islands have is developed at every stage of their school education.

Finlay MacLeod:
This is only the very beginning. But what is notable about the

Bilingual Project is that it has been doing so well, that the team is so extremely capable and, as an example, it holds a special position in showing everyone the way in which a renewal can be achieved.

PART THREE: The Media

The announcement of the project by the Scottish Education Department in July 1975 was greeted with a little flurry of publicity and the project got under way in September unnoticed by the media. However, the initial flurry heralded a blizzard of publicity which increased during the three years. The project was criticised, described, summed up, praised and commented upon in various ways from many viewpoints in newspapers, periodicals, on radio and television. Local political parties took up stances in relation to the project though none had visited the offices or discussed it with the team. Churches commented on it. Councillors cast the project about in debate but only two or three called in at the offices. Journalists and others filed lengthy articles about it. When in 1977 and 1978 the Council's Bilingual Policy was being discussed and debated publicly, it seemed that for many people the project *was* the Policy. Yet the project issued no press releases no statements, canvassed no journalists, sought no interviews.

In the first year the project featured in three television programmes and three radio programmes, one of which was wholly devoted to the project, being a 25-minute interview with the project director. Excluding the initial publicity already referred to, the project appeared in about ten newspaper articles; it was given prominence in "The New Edinburgh Review" No 33 and described briefly in the bilingual book "Gaidhlig ann an Albainn/Gaelic in Scotland" (Thomson 1976)[9].

It is interesting to note that most of the publicity was explanatory or informative, neutral in tone, and that most of the newspaper coverage was in Scottish national newspapers and internationally syndicated articles. While the "Scotsman" and the "Times Educational Supplement (Scotland)" gave considerable space to researched articles, and cuttings came to the project offices from the "Johannesburg Star", "San Francisco Chronicle" and "New York Times", there was scarcely any attention from the local newspapers.

The next year, the project attracted greater attention: in all, it was the subject of, or appeared in four television programmes, seven radio programmes and at least 28 newspaper articles or letters. It was also featured in the "Language Planning Newsletter", noted in the book "Language, Education and Social Processes in a Gaelic Community" (MacKinnon 1977)[10], and in the "BBC World Broadcasting Newsletter" (No 25) the project was listed as an agency influencing broadcasting.

Radio coverage that year included interviews for the BBC World Service and for the Canadian Broadcasting Service, Gaelic interviews and a 15-minute talk by the director about the work of the project. The television programmes were particularly interesting. For inclusion in a new series of programmes for children — "Cuir Car" — on Grampian Television, children and teachers in project schools were filmed and spoken to as they carried out some of the work being undertaken as part of their involvement. These programmes, which were broadcast on Saturday mornings, were very well received and gave children, parents and others an indication of the project in action, which they would not otherwise have had,

In the newspapers, the pattern of the previous year was changed, the bulk of the coverage being in two local weekly papers, the "Stornoway Gazette" and the "West Highland Free Press". National notice now attached to particular events such as the publication in August 1977 of the *Cliath* series although the stories usually attempted to provide some background information as well.

The "West Highland Free Press" and the "Stornoway Gazette" both covered the *Cliath* publication and the former included a lengthy and considered review of the books. Their main concern, however, was with bilingualism and bilingual education which were becoming very much public issues in the islands where, only a few years earlier, they were not publicly discussed. The Islands Council had formulated a draft Bilingual Policy and invited public comment, the activities of the project were becoming better known and the project, as the most noted example of bilingual development in practice, attracted a great deal of comment. The "Stornoway Gazette" carried 14 references in the period May—August 1977, including a 2,500-word article by the project director "Bilingual Education in the Western Isles", which was also printed in the "Inspectorate Bulletin" No 53 (Scottish Education Department, 1977), comment in a comprehensive essay "Bilingual Signs of the Times" by An t-Oll Urr Ruairidh MacLeoid and an article by Charles MacLeod, Head Teacher of a project school (Shawbost).

In the third year of the first phase, the project appeared in one television programme, six radio programmes and no less than 45 news-paper articles or letters. Apart from the programme transcribed in the preceding section of this chapter, radio and television coverage was in connection with the announcement of the second phase of the project, the forming of the publishing company Acair and publication of the *Spàgan* series. A brief outline of the project also appered in "The Older Mother Tongues of the United Kingdom" (James 1978)[11].

Whereas in the second year, most of the newspaper coverage of the project had resulted from the publication of the Council's Bilingual Policy, the focus in this third year was upon the project itself. As before, the national press reported and sometimes commented on the 'major' events and developments, which the local newspapers also reported. During that year, the possibility of bilingual primary education being introduced in Skye attracted considerable attention and some articles drew comparisons between the different approaches to bilingual education adopted in the Western Isles and in Highland Region. A report such as that in the "Aberdeen Press & Journal" (17/10/77) which, under the title "Gaelic-English teaching: Western Isles Lead the Way" alluded sharply to the different regional provision, highlighting the political minefield through which the project had to pick a discreet way.

Locally, the "West Highland Free Press" coverage included a report of the co-operation between the project and the University of Stirling to produce TV cassettes; a commentary on proceedings at a Scottish Educational Research Association conference, "Problems of Education in Remote or Sparsely Populated Areas" to which the project director had contributed; and an article entitled "The Environment is the Classroom," about a talk given by the project director to primary school teachers in Skye in February 1978. The most sustained exposure, however, was in the "Stornoway Gazette", which carried at least one comment, report or letter about the project in every issue but two in the three-month period from mid-December 1977 to mid-March 1978. The local Labour and Liberal parties issued statements about the Bilingual Policy — and the project. And a reader's letter headed "Non-Gaelic Speaking Children are Suffering", published before Christmas following the announcement of a second phase of the project stirred up a controversy that continued in the correspondence columns until the end of February. The project team did not participate in the debate, as usual.

In April 1978, the monthly community newspaper "News of the Isles" published in Uist carried an article by Annie MacDonald outlining the work planned for project schools during the summer term. The Gaelic 3-weekly newspaper, "Cruisgean", whose first issue appeared towards the end of 1977, published an article, assessing the progress of the project, written by Donald MacDonald, Head Teacher of a project school (Paible). Also, from March 1978 onwards "Cruisgean" has included regularly various writings by children in project schools.

Over the three years, then, the project attracted an unusual degree of attention in the media: 8 times on television, 16 on radio and at least 83 in newspapers, excluding brief or passing references which were far too numerous to record. Nobody could have anticipated the occurrence of such publicity in 1975: certainly the team did not.

With very few exceptions, the tenor of the coverage was favourable to the project. Bilingual education and the project itself were, for the most part, treated seriously in news, reports, articles, essays and correspondence columns. Occasionally, newspaper sub-editors, by attaching curious headlines to serious stories, must have puzzled their readers as much as they amused the team. "How the West was Won", for example, headed a report in the "Guardian" of publication of the *Cliath* series, "Cultivating Gaelic in the Garden" an article in the "Times Educational Supplement (Scotland)" on the environmental exploration encouraged by the project; and — most incongruously of all — the "Aberdeen Press & Journal" gave the title "Western Isles Scheme Aids Eskimo Language" to its report of a visit to the project office and schools in Lewis by representatives of the Labrador Inuit Association in 1976. However, frequent reports, explanations and interpretations of the activities and aims of the project in the media helped to bring the issue of bilingual education to public notice as well as generating an atmosphere of excitement about primary schools in the Western Isles. Partly as a result of the degree and quality of coverage, the project attracted a great number of visitors and reseachers from the islands, from mainland Britain and from overseas. Some of these visitors were educational day-trippers, but most were seriously interested or actively engaged in bilingual education; their contribution to the continuing formative thinking and discussion within the team was undoubtedly significant.

The team did not enter into public argument about the project; indeed, neither the team nor the teachers were the subject of publicity nor controversy. From the outset, the project had chosen a "low profile" approach. By the end of the first year it was clear that, while the project team and individual teachers might remain inconspicuous, the area of concern of the project was to become increasingly important in public esteem. It was important for the project to bring into the forum of public discussion issues, problems and attitudes concerning bilingual education and while the constant publicity subjected the team to pressure and necessitated the utmost discretion on their part, the overall effect of coverage in the media was beneficial to the project and to the development of bilingual education in the Western Isles.

PART FOUR: Reports and Records

The project team was involved in five kinds of written reporting, catering for different but not wholly separate audiences: the individual, the team, the Consultative Committee, the sponsoring bodies and the general public. In practice, however, most was reported to those who engaged most frequently in extended discussion with the team, the principal constraint being the confidentiality maintained by the team about its involvement with individual teachers and others.

Each team member kept a personal record or diary from the beginning. This record, usually in the form of rough notes, was not read by anyone else.

Because of the separation of the team, the multiplicity of its activities and the over-riding need to maintain close communication within the team, it was agreed at a very early stage that the research assistants would each prepare at intervals of about one month reports for circulation within the team but not beyond it. These reports, based upon the "raw material" of the personal records, summarised activity, indicated areas of apparent success for the team and teachers as well as areas of seeming failure. They also described practical and other problems, raised issues of concern and questions for discussion. Naturally, the team kept in touch from day to day by telephone discussions, in team meetings and through less formal conversations over cups of coffee. By itself, this would not have been enough. At a practical level, these reports kept the team informed of progress, of the salient issues, the waxing and waning of problems, as well as the activities and plans within the project. They kept the team's feet on the ground, focussed discussion on matters of central rather than peripheral importance and helped to develop within the project a disciplined, versatile intellectual thrust. For the individuals in the team, the necessity to compile considered reports encouraged regular reflection, at a remove from everyday concerns, upon aspects of the progress of the project and of their own involvement in it.

Beyond the team, the first audience was the Consultative Committee, whose meetings provided an extremely valuable forum for open, searching, sympathetic discussion and examination of all aspects of the project's work. The project director provided for the Committee a quarterly "Information Report", giving in a very condensed form a comprehensive review of activity in the preceding 13 weeks. At the end of the first phase, this amounted to a 75-page summary of activity. To these reports were regularly added press cuttings and other relevant information and, occasionally, detailed reports of specific matters. The Committee also required another kind of report dealing with issues, problems, plans, broad areas of concern in order that it might have an overall view of the direction in which the project was moving and be able to offer guidance to the team at this level. Accordingly, the project director prepared "Director's Reports" for the Committee.

The Committee already possessed information about activity in the project, ranging from financial or practical problems to current practice in classrooms or forthcoming publications, so the Director's Report concentrated on major issues or decisions arising from that range of activity. At some meetings where the morale of the team was compara- tively low, they sought to extract disproportionate joy — and praise — from a singular achievement, but never with any success: the Committee discussed issues and directions, not practical matters. Thus the compara- tively detailed personal records underwent processes of synthesis for and by different audiences so that what emerged had been honed down to a hard cutting edge: these processes are central to the kind of formative method of evaluation selected for the project, providing information for action.

The project also reported more briefly and formally to the Council and to the Scottish Education Department. These reports were on behalf of the team and the Consultative Committee and were, technically at least, available to the public. In September, 1977, for the Council and the Department, the project prepared an extensive document, "Interim Report, Submission and Estimates". This report of about 30 pages comprised an account of the project to that time and a detailed applica- tion for support of a second three-year phase.

For the fifth audience, the public, the team wrote a number of articles which are mentioned elsewhere in this report. They also contributed through interviews to written accounts prepared by others.

Of course, the team did not report only in writing and the project gave some account of itself at various stages to island audiences as well as audiences in Aberdeen, Glasgow, Inverness and Skye during the first phase. At meetings with teachers, meetings with other projects, repre- sentatives of institutions and agencies, seminars specifically dealing with reporting and on numerous other occasions, project team members took the opportunity to formulate, clarify or develop their ideas and their perception of the project.

Hoping that teachers, too, would welcome the opportunity to record their own activities and the progress of the project in their classrooms, the team issued to every teacher involved a loose-leaf notebook and asked them to build up their own diaries. It was explained that this diary would be of great value to the teacher herself both as a record of her involvement and a channel of communication to the team. The diaries would be collected into project centres periodically, photocopied and returned. Teachers were assured that in terms of the audiences delineated earlier in

71

this section, the diaries would be for the second audience only — the team. At the end of the first phase, the team had amassed in this way an enormous, heterogeneous collection of written reports from over 50 teachers in addition to information gleaned from meetings and personal discussion with them.

In the Interim Report already referred to, it is stated that teachers vary in the ways in which they maintain records of their work and that this is reflected in these diaries then available. At that time, it appeared to the team that only a minority of teachers were using the diary to its full advantage, to present the team with a blend of work in progress and comment of a particular or general nature. Most diaries provided a full record of work undertaken — in some cases, examples of work were appended — but, apart from occasional asides, did not include any comment. Some diaries, which provided neither a review nor comment, appeared to have been written in haste too long after the event. The Report states that "those who use their diaries most effectively are those who gain most, but the reliability of this kind of self-reporting has been questioned by many workers in the field of curriculum development."

In retrospect, this statement seems rather vaporous. The team was anxious from a very early stage about the reluctance of teachers to be as forthcoming in their written records as they were at meetings or in discussion of the project in their own classrooms. Was this because of memories of the "Record of Work" which teachers used to have to maintain and which was generally regarded as a worthless exercise? Was it because the team had not fully gained the confidence of teachers and were — in writing, at least — regarded only as enlightened missionaries of officialdom? Was it because people aware of the possibility of change do not want to record, for others, their own reactions to that? Certainly, for whatever reason, the diaries as a whole were more like circulars than letters, providing a great deal of very useful information in kaleidoscopic form about the project in action in school, but little direct comment from the teachers themselves.

It is undoubtedly true that too much stress is laid upon the written word as a method of reporting and of recording change. The clearest demonstration of the teacher's response may well be in the re-organisation of the furniture in the classroom, in the evidence of work emanating from the school, in the teacher's willingness to participate in group discussion, to become involved in her spare time in devising materials sought by the group. These, as well as the numerous photographs and the piles of school-produced materials in the project offices are as true reports as any written record.

6. Related Developments

In a previous chapter an account has been given of the developments that led to the formation of the publishing company Acair in the Western Isles. That this company had its origins in the project is clear, but not ultimately important. What is important is the relationship between Acair and the project and the effect of that relationship upon teachers and children in school. In this chapter, an account is given of several related developments which were affected by, and which in turn affect, the work of the project.

The Western Isles as a local government unit came into being in 1975, only five months before the project began. The newly formed Islands Council area brought together islands which had previously been administered by two separate mainland authorities, Ross & Cromarty and Inverness-shire. Bearing in mind that of the total population of approximately 30,000, 81.6% are bilingual, it is not surprising that the Council chose to be known by a Gaelic name — Comhairle nan Eilean — nor that one of its earlier declarations was of a Bilingual Policy by which the two languages of the community should enjoy equal status. This policy was formulated over the next two years and after a lengthy process of public consultation, a comprehensive policy was adopted by the Council in March, 1978. The project contributed directly to the formulation of the policy through the attendance of the director at meetings of the Programme Group set up by the Council for the purpose. The project also affected public reaction to the proposed policy during the period of consultation, because it was acknowledged in public statements by the Council to be the single most important step taken towards development of bilingualism in the area. Reciprocally, the formulation, consultation and adoption of the policy affected the project by heightening general awareness of bilingual education and in other ways discussed in the preceding chapter.

First phase 1975-78   John Murray

The paragraphs in the Bilingual Policy (1978) on primary school were:

3.2.3   "The specific aim of the Council in the provision of primary
education is that wherever possible Gaelic speaking children be
as literate and fluent in Gaelic as in English when transferring
from primary to secondary education and that the Gaelic speaking child's fluency and literacy in Gaelic be commensurate with
his or her fluency and literacy in English. In their first years at
primary school, Gaelic speaking children will be taught to speak,
read and write both Gaelic and English so that they will be able to
use both languages as a means of learning. Thereafter adequate
time and resources will be devoted to both languages, at all stages
of primary schooling to enable children to become fully bilingual.

The Bilingual Project, which is jointly sponsored by the
Council and the Scottish Education Department and is working
in twenty primary schools, has as its general aim the introduction
and development for children from a Gaelic-speaking background of a curriculum whereby they can learn through Gaelic as
well as English. The second three year phase of the Project will
cover the period up to September 1981 and will concentrate on
the dissemination of materials and methods to primary schools
not previously involved in the Project."[12]

One of the tasks originally set out for the team was "to provide
in-service courses for teachers engaged in the project." The team began
this task on the basis of the needs of schools, but inevitably became
involved with agencies and institutions outwith the area. There are two
very important factors which, ideally, should be taken into account in the
professional training of teachers coming to work in an area such as the
Western Isles: the rural, sparsely populated nature of the area and the
predominant bilingualism of the population. However, for various
reasons, comparatively little attention was paid to these by colleges of
education. Jordanhill College had a Gaelic department, but none provided courses on bilingualism, on the aims and different kinds of
bilingual education programmes, the psychological and linguistic development of the bilingual child, or bilingual classroom and school
organisation.

As has been described earlier, the project established teacher groups at
three levels — primary 1-3 teachers, primary 4/5 teachers, and primary
6/7 teachers — in Lewis/Harris and in Uist/Barra. Over the three years
these group meetings have enabled teachers to learn from the practice of
others, to seek group solutions to problems and to acquire a deeper
understanding of the needs of the bilingual children.

74

By means of these meetings and personal visits, a high degree of in-service training — continuous, flexible and relevant — has been provided for teachers participating in the project. Also, co-operation with the Education Department made it possible for the team to contribute directly to formal in-service training courses increasingly over the three years, so that in school session 1977-78 the principal concern of local authority in-service was exposition and dissemination of the work of the project. Team members have led courses by themselves or jointly with external tutors brought in for specific purposes; and, significantly, project school teachers have also participated as group leaders at courses.

By arrangement with Jordanhill College, a small number of student-teachers carried out part of their teaching practice in project schools in 1976, maintaining close contact with the project team during the three-week period. Everybody concerned deemed the experiment worthwhile and it was repeated in the next two years. The practice is now an accepted part of College provision. This venture pointed the way to building up — in the absence of provision of courses referred to above — a pre-service training course based upon and contributing to bilingual education in the Western Isles with purposeful liaison between the colleges and the local area. In internal reports and in published documents in 1977, the project sought to focus attention on the vitally important matter of pre-service training.

During the early months of 1978, the project participated in discussions involving Aberdeen College of Education and the local Education Department. The College, the Scottish Education Department and the Council all agreed that the College and the Council should, jointly, appoint a Bilingual Tutor/Lecturer who would be based for the greater part of each year in the Gaelic areas, spending the rest of the year at the College. The person appointed would be concerned with devising and implementing appropriate pre-service training for teachers in bilingual areas, working in close collaboration with the project. The post was advertised towards the end of the period of this report and at the end of September 1978, Miss Catherine MacDonald was appointed. This development is obviously of great importance for the project in its second phase and is also of some significance at national level for teacher training in general.

In 1975, the BBC began to broadcast on a regular basis two series of radio programmes in Gaelic for schools in North and West Scotland: *Culaidh Mhiogais* for children aged 5-7 and *Co Iad?* for children aged 8-10. For teachers in schools, this provided an important and valued resource and the project team was very keen to establish a good working relationship with the series producer as soon as possible. This was done, with the result that in the course of the three years of the first phase it became possible to co-ordinate series of programmes with the activities of the project in school. For example, in 1977, after consultation with the project, the BBC broadcast in *Co Iad?* a Gaelic adaptation of the novel "Hill's End" by Ivan Southall. The project issued to schools the original English novel and through meetings with teacher groups, the potential of the book as a basis for local studies was explored. Thus, in the schools, the teacher was able to make full use of the English novel and of a Gaelic adaptation as bases for a variety of language development and other creative work as well as a stimulus for social studies in the neighbourhood of the school.

Poems and rhymes from the project have been included in the *Culaidh Mhiogais* series and published in the accompanying "Teachers' Notes" (providing, incidentally, copyright and royalty income for project funds at Jordanhill College); the project provided wall-posters to accompany health education programmes and local history programmes in the *Co Iad?* series; and staff from the BBC, the local authority and the project have worked as a group at formal in-service courses for teachers. At the end of the first phase, it was evident that this co-operation would be extended and developed.

From the beginning, the project team sought to become conversant with developments in bilingual education nationally and internationally; through journals and reports, by correspondence with those involved and personal discussion whenever possible. During the first phase useful contact was established with agencies and projects in Ireland, Wales, France, Norway, Malaya, Australia, New Zealand and Canada as well as a range of developments in the USA. It was found that in some basic respects the project coincided closely with the 1968-77 Bilingual Education Project in Wales for example, in that the project "does not operate by interrupting the child's general education in order to insert Welsh lessons into the timetable; it uses Welsh as well as English as a medium . . ." (Price and Dodson 1978)[13]. The emphasis in the Western Isles project on exploiting the resources of the environment, however, is not present in the Welsh project, but is very similar to the practice in the Norwegian project based in the Lofoten Islands. Thus, from its earliest days, the project built up an international frame of reference, establishing a continuing exchange of information on a wide front. The team in its thinking and planning was in this way informed by the experience of others and an extensive range of relevant literature was made available for teachers to consult.

As the first phase of the project progressed, public discussion in Highland Region about Gaelic in education intensified. In the Isle of Skye, there seemed to be a growing concern about the decline of Gaelic and a desire for intervention to support the language at primary school level. The Highland Region Education Authority conducted a survey of parents in February 1978 to seek their views on the need for bilingual education at primary school. As a result, the Authority decided to introduce an experimental programme of bilingual education in 6 primary schools in Skye and two experienced teachers were appointed for this purpose in August, 1978. Annie MacDonald from the project team spent two days in Skye soon afterwards, in discussion with those full-time workers, visiting the schools concerned and talking to teacher groups about the Western Isles project. The project director had addressed a meeting of primary teachers and visited schools in February at the invitation of the Gaelic Adviser for Highland Region. Continuing contact between these projects will be mutually beneficial.

The Community Education Project, which is wholly funded by the Bernard van Leer Foundation, began a feasibility study in 1977 and entered its main 3-year phase early in 1978. The project was planned within the Education Department of the Western Isles Islands Council in consultation with the Bilingual Education Project and other bodies such as the Scottish Education Department and the University of Aberdeen. The broad aim of the project is to make a range of education resources available to the people of the Western Isles to equip them to tackle common problems more effectively and to enable them to live fuller lives in their communities. The project aims to help the individual principally by encouraging learning and action in a group setting. Its base, therefore, is in the community outwith the school, but its area of concern — like that of the community itself — encompasses the school.

Clearly, the Bilingual Education Project and the Community Education Project are linked by a broad area of common interest. Contact and co-operation between them has been close. In order to achieve an efficient working relationship it was essential for both project teams to have a firm understanding of the aims, objectives and strategies of the other project and numerous meetings took place between the teams during the period of this report. The projects have co-operated in material production, at in-service courses, in work with pre-school playgroups, in trying out local historical material in schools and in other ways. On a number of occasions, the projects have organised joint team seminars with discussion leaders from elsewhere, such as David MacKay — who after completion of the Feasibility Study for the Community Education Project, continued to offer a valuable consultancy to both project teams — Professor Karl Jan Solstad of Tromso University and David Hamilton of Glasgow University. The projects share the view that it is most important for team members to be put in situations which encourage reflection and to have to give accounts and reports of various kinds on their activities.

In 1978, the projects jointly prepared a case-study[14] of community and cultural education development in the Western Isles at the invitation of Dr Jonathan P Sher, then Director of the National Rural Center, Washington, for the OECD/CERI international project on Basic Education and Teacher Support in Sparsely-Populated Areas.

In October, 1977, a two-year Community Cinema and Video Communication Project, known as Cinema Sgire, began operation in Uist. Both the Bilingual and Community Education project staff were involved in early discussion and planning of this project which was sponsored by the Western Isles Islands Council with the Scottish Film Council, the Gulbenkian Foundation and the Highlands and Islands Development Board.

The video capability of Cinema Sgire is of particular interest to the Bilingual Education Project. A primary aim of Cinema Sgire is to encourage individuals and groups to use the video equipment to depict aspects of the community, to raise issues, to examine problems existing in the community. Preparation of any such video programme necessitates a thorough exploration of whatever first prompted the idea of a programme, careful formulation and structure, discussion of its possible use when complete and courses of action thereafter. Naturally, the Bilingual Education Project, which was engaged in encouraging a broadly similar process in schools, sought to co-operate with Cinema Sgire from its inception, to engage its resources in the classrooms. Children and teachers have made video programmes on archaeological sites and on mapping of the locality and teachers on one occasion made a programme for parents, showing some of the work on which they were currently engaged.

Fir Chlis, the first Gaelic professional theatre company, was registered in 1977. An experienced Gaelic-speaking artistic director and a full-time administrator were appointed in March, 1978, actors and technical staff in July, 1978. The company attracted finance from a number of sources, the principal funding bodies being the Scottish Arts Council and the Western Isles Islands Council in whose area the company was based. At the end of the first phase of the project, Fir Chlis had just begun its first tour which would take it to village halls and schools throughout the Western Isles. The company in its work in schools hopes to complement the work of the project and initial discussions took place in September, 1978 about the ways and means of achieving this.

The inter-relation of the Community Education Project, Cinema Sgire and the Bilingual Education Project is reflected, structurally, in the membership of their respective Consultative Committees. The project is represented on the Board of Directors of Acair, the Board of Governors of Fir Chlis, and the Schools Broadcasting Council (Scotland) Gaelic

Advisory Committee. It has also contributed directly since June, 1976 to the work of the National Committee on Primary Education Sub-Committee on Environmental Studies. Naturally, the project does not participate in these in any narrow way, but its principal purpose in becoming involved in the work of any other conterminous development is always to seek to make more resources available for children and their teachers in an area of great need and rising expectations.

7. Unfulfilled Demands

It will be clear that the project achieved a considerable amount in its first three years as well as setting courses, creating networks by which further, medium and long-term gains could be made. The setting up of such a project in a community created ripples, its very existence generating reactions and demands. It is evident that the project sharpened the teachers' perception of the children's needs and, naturally, this enhanced perception led to teachers making demands upon the project and upon the local authority. Pressure was increasingly put upon the team as a result of its own raising of aspirations among teachers and others and undoubtedly some urgent, important demands were not met in the first phase. For instance, the unprecedented flow of books and other printed materials into project schools generated demands for more and more books, the unprecedented level of consultation with teachers created demands for more consultation, participation in conferences gave rise to increased invitations, requests for greater participation, and so on. At this stage it is useful to indicate some of the most important of these areas of need which the project was not able to tackle sufficiently in the course of its first phase.

There are very few classrooms in the Western Isles in which all the children are Gaelic-speaking, although the vast majority of children are native speakers: in the 20 project schools, approximately 90% of the children come from Gaelic-speaking homes and have some knowledge of Gaelic. The project concentrated upon meeting the needs of the children who were already bilingual by enriching the primary school curriculum as a whole and insofar as it was successful in this, it is of benefit to all pupils, but no materials were produced specifically for teaching Gaelic either to native speakers or to non-Gaelic children. As the educational value of the project rose in the estimation of teachers, questions about effective classroom organisation to meet the linguistic needs of *all* the children began to be directed at the team. It is interesting that the very concern which had given rise to the project in the first place should emerge in this way from classrooms in relation to the need of non-Gaelic children to benefit from bilingual education.

The problem is partly, but by no means wholly one of organisation. A teacher may have three classes in the room including all or some of three distinct language groups — native speakers of Gaelic; non-Gaelic children who at their parents' request, are learning Gaelic; and non-Gaelic pupils whose parents do not wish them to learn Gaelic. The team attempted to help individual teachers in various ways to cope with this difficult situation and it is clear that teachers have, to a considerable extent, overcome the problem in the short term. It must be said, however, that the project provided no satisfactory long-term solution to these difficulties in its first phase.

The question raised in the preceding paragraph highlights the necessity for wide-ranging discussion involving national and local education authorities, schools and the community at large about the function of the school in a bilingual community such as that of the Western Isles, a "minority culture" community encompassed by a majority culture national community. It is possible for a school in the Western Isles to be thriving in terms of the wider community whose culture, values and language are dominant and at the same time by concentrating upon these alone to be — inadvertently — degrading and ultimately destroying the immediate community which it was built to serve. And that with the acquiesence, if not the wholehearted support, of the progressively debilitated population. The way in which schools in bilingual communities find a balance between these national and local considerations is of the utmost importance.

The project, operating within the school curriculum, is engaged in forging links between school and community in such a way that creative discussion and interaction is becoming possible. Parents and others have been able to participate in and contribute to learning activities in immediate, significant ways, whether as interviewees or as experts in their own right about various aspects of the environment or the life and work of the community. In an attempt to enhance this climate of mutual respect founded on knowledge rather than the lack of it, the project team held meetings with parents in eight of the project schools in the course of the first phase. Most of the meetings took place in the evening and were fairly lengthy — one or two lasted about four hours — and at all of them, the desire of parents to know more about what happens in school was obvious, as was their general approval of the project. Transmission of this real interest on the part of the parents into active participation, in the absence of regular contact between the school and parents of its pupils, would require a continuing series of such meetings impossible for the project team to sustain. It is interesting that in all but two of the meetings, the project team member was placed alone in front of parents, the school staff seating themselves among the parents. Growing doubts in the project about these meetings by themselves as a means of actively involving parents led the team to concentrate upon encouraging schools, by displays of their work and other approaches, to open out to the community.

One of the ways in which parents can gain confidence and acquaint themselves with their children's needs and the structures through which to seek satisfaction of these is by becoming directly involved in their children's education as early as possible. The project has sought to increase the contact between playgroup and primary school by arranging exchange visits in Ness (Lewis) in 1978, as well as by issuing materials to playgroups — both in co-operation with local authority departments and the Community Education Project. The exchange visits were effective as first steps in the right direction but further development at this important juncture of child, parent and teacher interests was not possible in the first phase.

Similarly, the project was involved in initiating discussion about appropriate provision in secondary school for bilingual children, and especially for the children who would be emerging from project schools into secondary education after several years of bilingual education. The project director and Council officials took part in a meeting with Principal Teachers of the Nicolson Institute, the only six-year school in the Western Isles, in February 1978. At the end of this lively meeting, it was agreed that a co-ordinating body should be set up to facilitate implementation of the Council's Bilingual Policy in secondary education and that information be made available to school staff about bilingual provision in secondary education elsewhere.

Through its national and international contacts, the project had access to a wide range of information and expertise in the field of bilingual secondary school education. In May, 1978, the project invited Mr Gerald Morgan, Head Teacher of a bilingual comprehensive school in Wales, to discuss bilingual secondary schooling with the teams of the Bilingual and Community Education Projects and officials of the Education Department. By arrangement with the Rector, Mr Morgan addressed a meeting in the Nicolson Institute and answered questions on organisation and other matters. The meeting was attended by the school staff, some Councillors and officials as well as all three project teams. The following day Mr Morgan spoke to the Lewis Head Teachers Association, also on Bilingual Secondary Education in Wales.

Again, a beginning was made and the project was actively involved in this; again a major area of concern far beyond the current capability of the project was indicated, a demand generated and expressed. For the project, it is essential not to be tempted to try to solve every problem, meet every demand, respond to every criticism — that way lies an erratic and brief career. However, while the importance of rousing issues, raising expectations and generating demands is generally acknowledged to be a major function of curriculum development projects, the task of enabling the satisfaction of demands, of meeting expectations and fully discussing issues requires much more in the way of staff and resources than the project was able to deploy.

8. Into the Second Phase

The climate in which the project operates has changed significantly since September 1975. At national and regional levels there is increasing interest in the Gaelic language, in its place in education, in the function and systems of community education and in the need to co-ordinate educational provision with community development.

The Western Isles Islands Council now has a comprehensive Bilingual Policy. The Highland Regional Council established a special sub-committee to consider in detail the role and responsibility of the Council in fostering Gaelic and subsequently placed substantial funding at the disposal of the sub-committee. An experimental scheme of bilingual primary education is under way in Skye. The Central Committee on the Curriculum invited observations from interested bodies regarding provision for Gaelic in the national curriculum development structure and it appears likely that an appropriate central committee will be established. The Highlands and Islands Development Board, by its vigorous promotion of community co-operatives, its involvement in such ventures as Acair and Fir Chlis and its adoption of a bilingual format for its own magazine, "North 7", is demonstrating a significant shift of emphasis in its approach to community development and education. Grampian Television has broadcast children's programmes in Gaelic — the first ever. The BBC has extended provision for Gaelic on radio and intends to broadcast on television a series of programmes with appropriate support material for those who wish to learn the language. In the field of teacher training, Aberdeen College and the Islands Council have taken the important step of appointing a full-time Bilingual Tutor/Lecturer.

Thus established bodies, since 1975, have instituted or are instituting changes which, taken as a whole, will affect profoundly the background to the project's second phase. These developments and innovations, together with the work of the other agencies operating locally, will affect attitudes, impinge upon the school curriculum and, in general, influence the project to degrees which cannot be gauged at present. Retention of the resourceful flexibility of approach which was developed in the initial phase is, therefore, essential.

The main priorities for the second phase, apart from the consolidation of advances already made, are the gradual extension of the project to include other schools in the Western Isles, greater active participation by parents and the community and continued preparation of appropriate materials. The strategies for consolidation, dissemination and extension in the second phase reflect the procedures which proved most successful during the project's first three years. Central to all of these will be the development of discussion among teachers, of facilitative groups and structures. The programme as a whole is aimed at building up individual and team strengths in the original 20 schools to enable teachers in these schools to take over a leading role in dissemination and in encouraging an innovative approach among their colleagues. At the same time, the team will try to ensure that schools not hitherto involved have access to the necessary background information and that a receptive, willing attitude obtains.

This report, which can be regarded as "final" only in a very artificial sense and which will itself be one of the factors affecting the project in its second phase, is an account of work in progress, of beginnings. At this stage, however, it is possible to tease out from the complex, evolving pattern of activity some of the main strands of development which will strengthen the project in its second phase.

Attention has been focused on the special qualities and needs of bilingual children; the status and the use of Gaelic in school have been improved and extended; a bilingual mode of teaching and learning has been introduced and partially developed. And teachers as well as the team are satisfied that these developments have not been in any way at the expense of English — some teachers and others maintain that the nature of the work encouraged by the project has improved the children's fluency and range in both languages. The Council's Bilingual Policy, in the section on education, took into account the aims and practice of the project, so that integration of these into local authority provision is facilitated.

Through its emphasis on making full use, at all stages of primary school, of the rich educational resources of the physical, cultural and social environment of the school, the project has begun to ensure that learning in school is relevant to living in the community as well as to the wider aspirations of pupil, parent and school. The content of the curriculum has been augmented and enriched. An experimental approach on the part of teachers has been encouraged.

Public awareness of bilingual education and of the school curriculum has been increased. Parents and others in the community have begun to contribute directly to the school curriculum as well as to the continuing public discussion of bilingualism and bilingual education. Similarly, the project has brought the position in the Western Isles to the attention of agencies and institutions in the UK and abroad, gaining access to the findings of others and contributing to international discussion of bilingual education.

An unprecedented flow of Gaelic books and other materials into schools has begun. In the case of published books, great care was taken to ensure that text, illustration and design were appropriate to current needs and that the book itself was of a high standard of production. Preparation of printed and audio-visual materials other than these is well-established, with teachers and their classes playing an increasing part in all stages of the process. The setting up of the publishing company Acair will assist greatly in this field, as well as in general educational development.

Teacher groups of various kinds have met frequently, so that the professional isolation which many rural teachers bear has been overcome to some extent. These groups and individual teachers are becoming more confident, gradually assuming greater responsibility for material preparation, for curriculum planning and development. The work of the project has formed the basis of several in-service courses. Project school teachers have begun to participate as discussion leaders at such courses.

The pre-service training of teachers to work in bilingual schools, while it still falls far short in many respects of what is required, is changing. Jordanhill College incorporates some of the project's findings into its training and sends students annually to carry out part of their teaching practice in the Western Isles. Aberdeen College, jointly with the Western Isles Islands Council, has appointed a Bilingual Tutor/Lecturer to devise and implement courses based principally upon the experience of the project.

Links with individuals and agencies together with mutually supportive networks of interested bodies have strengthened the project as well as extending its sphere of influence and disseminating its practice.

In personal growth, development of skills and in many other ways, the project team has itself gained much from working closely with teachers and pupils and from the many activities which this involvement necessitated. Most teachers, like the team, accept that for everyone concerned, involvement in the project is a learning process.

Second Phase 1978-81
Catherine Morrison

1. The Project Continues

In view of the considerable measure of success experienced in the first 3 years and the vital tasks identified as remaining unfulfilled, a submission requesting extension of the project for a further 3-year period was granted the approval of both the funding bodies. Comhairle nan Eilean increased its financial input to £96,450 to cover the 3 years. The Scottish Education Department maintained its previous level of grant which amounted to £40,347 for the new phase. The Local Authority was now bearing the greater part of the costs, and this was in line with SED's policy of phasing out its own financial support. Administrative arrangements continued as before. The director and secretary were employees of Jordanhill College and paid out of the SED grant, while the salaries of the seconded research assistants/fieldworkers were accounted for in Comhairle nan Eilean's share of the budget.

The second phase of the project was to run for 3 years from September 1975-1981. Its main aims were:—

a)   consolidation and further development of work begun in the original 20 schools;

b)   extension to other primary schools in the Western Isles;

c)   continued production of Gaelic materials.

It had already become apparent that if the project were to expand its activities, the team would require to be enlarged. In recognition of this need, Comhairle nan Eilean had, in June 1978, agreed to second another teacher to the team. It was hoped that another additional member could be added to the team later but in point of fact this did not prove possible. The team therefore operated under-strength throughout the second phase.

The project team has had some continuity of staffing but it has also undergone some staffing changes. At the end of the first phase, John

Murray left, and was replaced by Catherine Morrison as director. In Uist, Annie MacDonald was joined by Effie MacQuarrie a research assistant in Uist/Barra. Christina Mackenzie was appointed as the research assistant for Lewis/Harris schools. Later, the vacated post of secretary was filled by Joan Alice Matheson.

Neither was staffing constant in the schools. Some considerable turnover took place in project schools due to teachers retiring, going on leave for a time or leaving the islands. Work continued with the 20 first phase schools and a further 14 were included, bringing the total number of project schools in the second phase to 34.

The Consultative Committee agreed that evaluation of the project should continue as before, forming an integral part of the work. In view of the wide-ranging nature of the development task and the very many variables involved, it was felt that an on-going formative type of evaluation was the best suited method. It would be undertaken by teachers and the team who would continually assess and record progress being made, seeking to define and analyse problems and finding ways of overcoming them. A summative account would be produced at the end of the project.

2. The Curriculum

At the time that the project entered the scene in 1975, primary school education in the Western Isles, in common with other areas of the country, was in the process of undergoing a very gradual but radical change. Ten years previously the Scottish Education Department had produced its new memorandum of advice and guidance in the form of 'Primary Education in Scotland'[3], a statement which "took account of contemporary advances in education, child psychology, and the society around them . . ." In the wake of its publication, new approaches to learning were being advocated by Local Authorities and tried out in the schools, the basic principle being that learning was to be made more relevant to the needs of the child, with more account being taken of his background and environment. With the schools then beginning to enjoy improved facilities and the increased availability of attractive resource materials and modern technological aids, learning situations were being made more stimulating, so that on the whole, teaching was becoming a more pleasurable if demanding and challenging experience. The standard of education in general appeared to be moving towards a state of advancement and improvement.

It was of course natural to expect that practice would vary from one classroom to the next. There were teachers who favoured the new methodology more than others, just as some had been better-placed to benefit from the guidance and in-service training given. In the nature of things, each learning milieu has its own particular set of variables some of which may facilitate progress or on the other hand hinder it. Consequently different effects are produced. The identification of the underlying causes which account for these differences in goals and achievements is of the utmost importance. The causes are many and are often complex and interesting.

In setting out to design the new approach to learning through Gaelic, the project team along with teachers gave considerable thought to what would likely be the most effective method of developing the children's capabilities. Account was taken of the evidence available on the way children naturally begin to acquire language even almost from birth. Their learning of language is geared to their needs, assisting them to order their world about them, to interpret their experiences to themselves and others. In this way their language learning is linked to their development of concepts, the one being mutually dependent on the other. The team were of the opinion that the role of Gaelic in school should similarly be as a tool for learning and describing of experience. By using their two languages as media of exploration of the world about them, their learning would be enriched. And, of course, the function the Gaelic language would have would be very much dependent on the content and teaching method employed.

Accordingly, the project advocated linking development of Gaelic in school with the children's interests and experience. Consideration was also given to discovering appropriate methods to assist them in interpreting and clarifying their experiences. The project believed that one of the most effective ways of doing this would be through pupils pursuing direct investigations of varied aspects of their own environment under the guidance of their teachers, part of whose role would be to seek to ensure that the learning was being adequately extended and enriched. New learning would be based on what children already knew and understood, using this as a springboard for explorations of other environments. The team accepted this principle as being fundamental to the child's real understanding of concepts, and the learning and application of skills.

For some teachers, the idea of using the local environment as a teaching resource was not a novel experience, though there were others who, to begin with, questioned its value. Previously the inclusion of local content in the curriculum had not been given high priority. The school had therefore in a sense served to alienate children from their own culture and background. The project believed that the local environment provided an excellent medium for direct investigations, and that gaining knowledge about the past and present of their own community would help to instil in the pupils a much-needed sense of identity and confidence in themselves as people, and would help to foster in them an interest in and sympathy with the affairs of their own locality.

When devising ways by which to put its objectives into practice, the project considered it to be fundamental to discover what the children's needs were at all stages of the work. The team was from the outset conscious of the need to work closely with the children and teachers in the schools. Since the means of access to the children was indirectly through the teachers, it was of first importance to discover how the teachers perceived the children's needs and what their own attitude was to the planned change. Only through a positive and willing attitude on the part of the teachers could the project be given a fair trial. Moreover, if the project were to have a lasting effect teachers had to be encouraged to take an innovating role themselves. The project was set up as a new resource for teachers to help them in their self-development as effective practitioners of a bilingual curriculum. Thus the project has throughout its life been as much concerned with adult education as with the education of the children.

So, the establishing of close working relationships between the team and the teachers was seen as being of crucial importance to the project. In an atmosphere of mutual trust and respect, teachers were more inclined to express their feelings and experience, and not feel threatened by the new venture, although on occasion there were one or two who tended to see the project as questioning their professional capability and autonomy. Teachers on the whole were frank and open in their comments, airing opinions and criticism as the need arose. Constructive criticism enabled the team to give advice and guidance as necessary. It was much more difficult for the fieldworker to find a base from which to begin where criticism was usually negative or where little comment at all was forthcoming. Compared to the situation which existed at the beginning of the project, the standard of discussion on the curriculum among teachers rose markedly.

Although all the schools which were approached agreed to join the project, it was soon discovered that this did not necessarily signify that each and every teacher would automatically or even readily accept the proposed methods of teaching through Gaelic. This was to be expected. It was inevitable that many teachers would experience personal and organisational difficulties in committing themselves to the new approach. But the project structure had been set up to help resolve these and similar difficulties. Teachers were to be enabled to identify and articulate their problems, and with assistance to seek ways of overcoming them.

Many reservations were expressed. Some teachers felt parents would fail to understand why an increased amount of time should be spent on Gaelic and would look on excursions outwith the classroom as a waste of time. Some feared other areas of the curriculum would suffer as a result. Their main concern, they said, was to teach the basic skills and to prepare the children for Secondary Education and they doubted that the new bilingual approach would satisfy these demands. Other teachers were not confident of their own ability to use the environment as a teaching resource, in that they lacked specialist knowledge of its potential and therefore felt themselves to be inadequate in approaching it. The lack of relevant printed materials in Gaelic posed difficulties for them. Some considered that it would be more comfortable and more secure to continue the learning as before, using text-books in the classroom. Classes of mixed ability in Gaelic were viewed by a few as an obstacle. Yet, for other teachers, none of these issues presented problems of any significance.

There was no simple and quick method that the team could convincingly use to allay doubts and remove the problems perceived by the teachers. The process had to begin by encouraging and stimulating teachers to try out the project methods for themselves. Before long, the successful practice of colleagues provided proof and incentive to those who had been more dubious about its chances of success. Very gradually uncertainty gave way to increasing confidence as more and more teachers allowed themselves to experiment. Fresh insight was gained into how children learn and through their own changing perception, teachers began to have increasing awareness of what was of real educational value to their pupils.

Because of the complex and long-term nature of the change aimed for, it would have proved difficult for the individual teacher to sustain headway on her own without access to sources of consultation and discussion. However, these needs were being met through the organising of teachers group meetings and fieldworker visits to schools. In generating and testing fresh ideas in the schools, and in discussing this work with their colleagues and with the team, the teachers were developing the new curriculum.

Thus, teacher support and development has been a principal concern of the project. That support evolved and took various forms as the situation required. In the early stages the team gave close guidance, suggesting lines of development through discussion at meetings and during school visits, frequently following this up with guidelines in written form. On occasion the fieldworker would accompany a class on an excursion or give a demonstration lesson in the classroom if it was felt that this would strengthen the teacher. In this way the aims and rationale of the project were being put across to teachers through practical experience. Having seen purpose in the approach being advocated, teachers were enabled to apply it and innovate further for themselves.

From the start, the majority of teachers responded positively to the support of the team, welcoming and faithfully following the advice and guidance given. Happily, this led to their being convinced of its worth. They became more self-critical and able to discuss the work constructively. Gradually they grew to become more self-reliant so that less direct involvement was required of the team.

In the first phase, the team had initiated the work by selecting certain content through which schools could carry out explorations in Gaelic. The choice of content in itself was not regarded as being exclusively important, yet it had to satisfy certain criteria for it to have potential for the kind of classroom work being aimed for. The team worked with groups of teachers and selected a common theme for each group. It was decided to work with common themes since it would be easier to guide the early development work, and teachers would have more in common to compare and discuss.

At the end of three years, having taken the first broad strokes across the full primary age range, closely monitoring the development work done at each stage, it was evident that the teaching methods and content discussed through the means of the project were being adopted in the schools. Teachers were approaching the work with increasing confidence so that they now wished more autonomy in deciding their own content. This was a sign of progress welcomed by the team. The second phase therefore witnessed an overwhelming variety of themes being done through the medium of Gaelic.

In previous years with the phasing out of a narrowly prescribed scheme of work teachers had been granted considerable latitude in choosing curriculum content, particularly in the field of environmental studies. While this presented special opportunities, it could also prove daunting for some to be confronted with such a host of topics to choose from. The choice exercised by teachers often simply was continuing what they used to do, or adopting what publishers were promoting or what the local library was offering in centre of interest boxes, or whatever. While most of these offered good content in themselves they often did not satisfy the criteria of having a Gaelic and local component. Neither were some of them particularly conducive to child-centred learning.

Now, however, it was evident that teachers were developing expertise in selecting and carefully planning content to incorporate various skills and concepts. It was particularly encouraging to see how the curriculum now was more closely reflecting the children's environment and background. Successive new teachers to the project were beginning to absorb ideas and methods from their more experienced colleagues and from the team members.

While in the first few years of the project a vast amount of excellent work had been achieved through both languages, themes had been fairly loosely structured and planning of them had been a little haphazard. Being at an early stage of development, this was acceptable enough since the project was tentatively feeling its way forward and no real criticism could be levelled at the quality of the work. Besides, what had been of first importance was the creation of a stimulating learning and teaching environment; a positive atmosphere in which teachers could feel they were breaking new ground. As the project developed it recognised that there was a need for a more structured framework which would accommodate a proper balance of subjects, concepts, and skills, to ensure progression of learning experiences for the child throughout school.

The work of the Scottish Committee on Environmental Studies (SCES) was being developed at this time, and one of the project fieldworkers was a member of that committee. In this way the foremost ideas being developed at national level were incorporated into the project and offered to teachers at school level. This approach sought to clarify the balance and progression in this work throughout the school.

The SCES view was that:—

"School policy in environmental studies should be designed to achieve a gradual development of . . . 6 basic Skills (both practical and attitudinal) and 9 basic Concepts . . . by means of an appropriate balance of content topics including health, history, geography and science."

This provided a useful handrail for teachers when formulating how a given theme was to be opened out for the children so as to provide numerous experiences in which to apply their 2 languages in writing, reading and speech.

With children, oral communication is a major instrument of learning. Teachers were in agreement that the developing of spoken Gaelic should be the first priority. They claimed that the children's Gaelic was of a poor standard, that their vocabulary was impoverished, and the cause of this they ascribed to parents not speaking much Gaelic to their children. It would be quite a task, they felt, for the teacher to achieve anything very much. The project discussed with teachers the urgent need to expose children to hearing a lot of Gaelic spoken in the school situation by their peers and by adults, and for activities to be devised which would encourage uninhibited spontaneous and varied expression and discussion. Due to the recent focus, nationally, on development of talk in school, much good teacher material was available to which the team referred teachers and which was used by fieldworkers as the basis for some meetings.

Once talk in Gaelic was utilised more in the new learning situation, teachers were pleased to discover how motivated children were to talk, and that their facility in Gaelic was considerably more than had been assumed. In developing spoken language, a different role was required of the teacher herself in that she was not asking 'closed' questions to test the children's knowledge: she was now acting more as a guide to children in their thinking, whether learning in the classroom or exploring outdoors, drawing attention to whatever was of significance and which might otherwise go unnoticed.

Thus, the range of uses of talk in Gaelic was being widened much more than formerly. In conjunction with other skills it was also used, for example, in seeking information through interviewing members of the community, in communicating experience through spontaneous dramatic play, in analysing and relating findings to others. In all its different functions, the focus was not on the language itself but on the use to which it was put. Children now had real purpose for talk and were more motivated to do so.

Many other skills, verbal and non-verbal, were used to express feelings, to search for information and then to communicate the information gleaned — skills of photography, art and crafts, mapwork, reference skills, etc. These skills were now being more systematically catered for and integrated with the rest of the learning. Often it was discovered that such skills were much more complex than at first appeared. To quote one example: when using English reference material for work in Gaelic, the child had to be able to listen or read and comprehend, extract the necessary information, and put it into Gaelic in communicating it either in oral or written form.

Compared with the formal, restricted kind of writing which used to be done, the range and quality of Gaelic writing throughout the primary school had been advanced. Teachers remarked that children had more to write, were more inclined to project their personal selves into the writing and could adapt to differing styles. Working from a base of confidence, discussion and shared experience children now had a sense of purpose and motivation.

In Gaelic writing, the problem most visible to teachers was not that the children had nothing to write about, but that they were not technically equipped to do so. For most teachers, the teaching of Gaelic spelling presented a major obstacle. Children were being helped to spell in English and there was plenty of material available for the purpose, but the teaching of Gaelic orthography to children had never been systematically dealt with. Furthermore, many teachers felt themselves at a disadvantage never having been taught it in school. Meantime, there was much the teachers themselves began to attempt. At the suggestion of the team or on their own initiative many willing teachers worked out ways of helping children with Gaelic spelling, and with encouraging results. They discovered that it was no longer the major handicap they had imagined it to be since children took it well in their stride. Needless to say there is still a tremendous amount to be done in this field.

The improvement in children's Gaelic writing can be attributed in some measure to their generally being introduced to it at an earlier age.

From the age of 5 or 6 children are encouraged to describe their experiences in writing as in other forms of expression. Because of their inability to handwrite and spell at this age, the teacher will write what the child wishes beneath his drawings, thus giving the child a sense of fulfilment and introducing him to the written word in a meaningful way. Since the early written work is the child's own composition it is of interest to him and he is more motivated to read it. For this purpose, the Gaelic adaptation of 'Breakthrough to Literacy' has proved a most useful tool. Much Gaelic material is compiled in classrooms in this fashion with children gradually gaining mastery of the technical skills.

Not all classrooms displayed a general improvement, nor were all pupils encouraged to express themselves through Gaelic writing. A few teachers did not themselves see value in it since they did not feel that lack of this skill would have any adverse effect on the child in later life. Other teachers felt inadequate in their ability to develop good quality creative writing. As was done with many other techniques the project deployed teachers with flair and skill in this aspect of the work to disseminate their practice to their colleagues. The standard of the writing was gradually being advanced as teachers became more discriminating in assessing its quality and finding ways of improving it.

Before the project, most of the time spent on the teaching of Gaelic had been devoted to learning to read. The usual practice was for all children to acquire the mechanical skill of reading through passages from a class reading book, followed by questions of interpretation. It was not unusual to come across a situation where the whole class, Gaelic and non-Gaelic children alike, read the same material, although often the non-Gaelic children could not comprehend what they were reading and had little facility in speaking the language. But for all, the opportunity for reading was scant, material was scarce, and most of what was available was limiting, inappropriate, and not particularly interesting.

Since the setting up of the project, there has been an increase in the amount of Gaelic material available, much of it having been generated by the project itself, with contributions being made by the children, the teachers, and the team. The establishment of the bilingual publishing company Acair has also induced other writers to produce books for use with children in the schools or in the home. The content, style and appearance of these books is more attractive, relevant, and varied, allowing much greater flexibility of use. Consequently children's reading of Gaelic is more purposeful so that their attitude to it and skill in it has been improved. In many schools however, children's skill in Gaelic reading does not yet match that of English. The supply of material is still quite insufficient, coupled with the fact that, outwith school, children have little exposure to the printed word in Gaelic.

Had the project been designed to rely solely on Gaelic books and books of local content to promote learning, it would have encountered serious difficulties. There was, and still is, little published material of this kind available, especially for the middle and upper ranges of the school. Doubtless this may have impeded progress, since the extraction of information from books is an important part of learning. But the project did not lean very heavily on text-book learning anyway, since implicit in its experiential approach was the use of alternative sources of reference from the environment.

So, throughout the 6 years, classes have made innumerable trips outdoors to study aspects of natural history, visit historical sites, learn about seasonal activity in the villages, examine economic aspects of the way of life, learn about the work of community co-operatives etc: all the while concerned with the how and why of things and using both the Gaelic language and English as media of learning. Information was also gathered from old photographs and documents in the archives of the local history societies and the local library. Members of the community were widely utilised as sources of reference, whether questioned and tape-recorded by children at home, brought in for talks in the classroom, or interviewed at work. In the process, the children's own environment, past and present, was being validated for them so that they were becoming more aware of its physical, social and cultural components.

The teachers' initial fears of their own lack of specialist knowledge began to disappear. They soon realised this lack was not a serious impediment since there was always an expert on hand to accompany them on their excursions to supply information, be it, for example, the professional expert in natural history, the worker in the seaweed factory, or the old lady who has spent her youth at the herring fishing. Such contacts to begin with were made at the instigation of the project team; later on teachers themselves took the initiative so that a countless number of members of the community have been involved in this way in the role of educators. For the pupils this kind of learning is motivating, enjoyable and educationally beneficial. Teachers also enjoy it, and learn with the children and develop fresh interests as a result.

Through implementing the approach described, it can be seen that closer links between the school and its community continue to be developed and strengthened. Many parents by participating in and contributing to the curriculum in informal ways were gaining better understanding of the school's activities, reacting favourably and with interest to the work of the project and wishing their children to benefit from bilingual education. It is but a beginning, however, and but one of the ways to be utilised for effecting co-operation between the school and the local community.

Almost from the outset the project has been under steadily increasing pressure from various sides to provide Gaelic education for children who have little or no knowledge of Gaelic. Practically every classroom has some proportion of pupils in that category. Teachers have expressed concern over problems of organisation in classes having a wide range of ability in Gaelic, with little material available suited to their needs. Parents of such children have expressed a desire to have them taught Gaelic. The team recognises that the need exists for a programme for children with little or no knowledge of Gaelic. The project, however, was set up to provide for the native Gaelic-speaking child, and this it considered to be its first priority.

But beginnings have been made. Individual teachers with the support of the team are trying out various approaches with the children. With young children, emphasis has been on their learning of language which is meaningful and which is linked to their activities. Simple reading material is also being prepared. Provision for older children has been largely in the form of the BBC Schools Gaelic series 'Toiseach Toiseachaidh' which is based on the bilingual method devised by professor Carl Dodson of Wales. The experience and findings of these approaches is being monitored and will be taken into account in the team's thinking out and devising of an appropriate approach for Gaelic second-language learners. Of itself, it will not necessarily solve the apparent organisational difficulties in the mixed ability classroom. But it is an approach which will be more appropriate to the needs of some of the schools still to be included in the project.

3. Extending the Project

By the end of the first phase, the project was operational throughout the whole primary age range in 20 schools. A good beginning had been made; much had been achieved, though much still remained to be done. In the phase ahead, the project saw its task in these schools as being to consolidate the gains already made and to further explore aspects of the bilingual curriculum which as yet were largely not touched upon.

But it was not to confine itself to these schools. Other schools were to be offered the opportunity to benefit from the findings and the experience gained. The project had already, in some measure, become more widely available through the published materials and through project exhibitions and in-service courses, so that many teachers in other schools were themselves attempting similar work in Gaelic. There was nonetheless a need for a more systematic programme of dissemination to allow those teachers to become more directly involved. Accordingly, in the second phase the project was extended to include 14 more schools. The project was now operating, broadly, two sets of schools in parallel, though the distinction could not always be sharply defined.

The main aims of the second phase were: consolidation in the original project schools, further extension to other primary schools, and continued production of materials.

It was usually found that for a teacher to become fully conversant with the approach of the project, that she had to experiment and experience for herself. In this way, many who to begin with were sceptical, uninterested, or mystified by the proposals of the team, soon discovered for themselves the real value and purpose of the work. The project's approach here relied on the psychological finding that one's attitude tends to change so as to be in line with one's actions.

Meetings of teacher groups were chosen as the forum for learning.

First phase teachers and their work provided a working synthesis of what had been achieved so far, encouraging new teachers to join in this venture. So the successful practice of those teachers stimulated others to learn through emulating, or by experimenting further for themselves. A setting providing personal interaction was felt to be necessary if teachers were to feel sufficiently secure in themselves to consider new ways of working.

The idea of 'teachers learning from teachers' was an important strand in the pattern of the project. Teachers' meetings provided the focal point for this learning to take place in a group setting. The dissemination programme was aimed therefore at enabling teachers to take the lead in helping others towards innovative work.

For this purpose, it was decided to form area 'clusters' of schools. The plan was that a well-established project school would form the nucleus of a cluster of schools in its surrounding area. Teachers in that school, through teacher-meetings at local level, would then become the disseminators of the project to other schools in the vicinity. The special strengths of these teachers would be identified and deployed at meetings to benefit others. In contrast to the way that the school had been gradually phased in the first three years, new schools would be brought in as complete units. It was anticipated that team members would also be involved in the meetings, at least in the early stages of the second phase.

The suggestion of area meetings received whole-hearted approval from teachers. It appeared that participation in a small more familiar group, was more appealing to teachers than wider exposure in a large group. Thus the professional isolation which can be experienced by teachers in 1-teacher schools and other small schools in remote areas would be broken down through their reaching out to other schools in their own locality. There was also the advantage of the amount of travel being lessened.

Four 'area clusters' were chosen: Ness, Harris, South Uist, Barra.

In the Ness area of Lewis there were four schools. Two of them were well-established project schools; all were feeder schools of the same secondary department. Also the Community Education Project was operational in that district. Ness seemed an obvious choice.

Since the project centres were located comparatively distant from Harris and Barra, fieldworker contact with these areas and teacher attendance at meetings tended to be more infrequent than was the case with other schools. It was felt that those two areas would benefit more from meetings being held in their own local area.

At about the time that planning of 'clusters' was being done, an in-service course on environmental science was being held for all South Uist schools by a visiting tutor. Featured as part of the course was a display of work from first phase schools with discussion of it by the teachers. In follow-up to the course teachers in all the schools were to carry out an assignment in environmental science. Knowing the desired approach to be in line with that of the project, teachers in the non-project schools there sought assistance of the team. It seemed an opportune time for the project to extend to those schools and so organise a cluster in the South Uist area.

In early 1979, by way of inviting new schools to join the project, team members visited the schools to introduce the idea to the staff and to discuss its implications. On the whole, teachers were interested, many of them questioning and discussing the implications at length. It was evident that the schools already had some knowledge of the approach being advocated by the project through having seen the publications, through attending in-service courses and having had informal contact with project teachers. It was also noticed that in a few instances some of these points of contact had given rise to some misconceptions as to the real nature of the work. Clearly it was seen that teachers would benefit from more direct participation with access to informed discussion and guidance. In general, the issues and problems raised were strangely reminiscent of first approaches to schools at the outset of the project. All schools agreed to participate.

In these initial discussions, teachers generally appeared in favour of Gaelic being part of the curriculum, but they stated that they were already doing Gaelic and that what was needed was more books and materials to help them with it. Some thought the project's chances of success were limited since the language was in decline among children and they believed that the parents and the media were largely to blame for this. A few teachers were concerned that it would add to the frustrations already experienced by them due to an overloaded time-table. Some had misgivings about the value of teaching Gaelic and about their own ability to do so. But others perceived great benefit in joining the project as a source for more material and guidance.

A further extension of the strategy for dissemination was to test the extent to which local cluster groups, once formed and familiar with the processes involved, could be maintained and run by the teachers themselves. To attempt this would show the extent to which fieldworkers could withdraw from regular attendance at each group, to a stance where they could respond to the needs arising from the whole range of local meetings taking place. It was not clear whether this could be achieved: the level of back-up required to enable the pattern of local meetings to occur was to be explored. The onus for development — both personal and in their work — was with the teachers. The project was there to facilitate that development.

The project's approach was complemented by the Education Department's programme of school-based in-service days under the guidance of the promoted staff in each school. This was going on in all the primary schools in the Western Isles, including the schools in the project. These within-school meetings which were aimed at developing school policy across the curriculum were seen as strengthening the project cluster meetings in that each individual teacher was being challenged to contribute to the overall attempt at developing a well-formulated relevant school curriculum. These school-based meetings used as a basis for consideration, the various reports of the Committee on Primary Education (COPE) as well as SED Reports such as 'The Education of Pupils with Learning Difficulties 1978, and 'Learning and Teaching in Primary 4 and Primary 7' 1980.

The second phase aimed to clarify the extent to which the 'good practice' — in planning and implementing a bilingual curriculum — which had evolved in the first phase could be further clarified and strengthened in the second phase schools. Essentially, at the level of the individual teacher in project schools, the second phase sought to clarify further the extent to which the bilingual schooling she was offering the children was the result of sustained planning and reflection on her part, in the light of her participation in within-school discussions and local 'cluster' groups of teachers set up within the project's second phase.

4. Materials

Accounts given elsewhere in this book highlight the continuing pressing need for resource materials in Gaelic to further extend and support the curriculum being developed. A considerable amount of material was produced and generated by the project in its first phase. Provision was further increased in the second phase.

As described in the First Phase Report, one major need identified by the project was an early reading scheme in Gaelic. So, in response to this need, a series of 24 books, now known as the 'Grian' books, was prepared by the project. These were designed in accordance with certain criteria which were considered appropriate for material for the teaching of reading. Thus it was felt to be important that the books should reflect the children's view of the world, that their vocabulary and interests should be taken into account, and that this could best be done by basing the content on their own oral accounts, their texts and illustrations. Before being sent out for publication, the prepared texts were given a period of trial in the schools, to allow any necessary refinements to be made, and to collect material from which final artwork could be prepared. Some initial delay was experienced in securing publication, due to the high costs involved in producing a 24-book series with 4-colour illustrations as was originally intended. Eventually the series was accepted by Acair who agreed to publish the books with costs scaled down to allow for 2-colour printing, and the series to be published six titles at a time.

In developing the area of early reading, the team favoured also the approach employed by 'Breakthrough to Literacy' which had been published in English (Longman Group) and which had been adapted into other languages. Some experimentation on a minor scale had already been successfully carried out with a Gaelic version of it in Western Isles schools. The team believed that this was a resource which could be used to great effect in teaching initial literacy to Gaelic-speaking children. Furthermore, the project was extremely privileged in having direct access for guidance to David Mackay, the creator of 'Breakthrough', who fortuitously was working in the Islands at the time.

Briefly, 'Breakthrough' is an early reading and writing scheme which "places the learner himself in continuous control of the language he is developing in order to become both a reader and a writer." (Breakthrough to Literacy Teacher's Manual, 1970, Longman). It provides the child from the time he is ready to read with materials which enables him to express himself in written language even before he has acquired the manipulative skill of writing. Since the language used is his own personal language, conveying his own vocabulary and his own interests, he is more motivated to learn to read it. The material basically consists of cards with words which have high frequency of use, a storage folder for the cards, and a plastic stand in which to set out the cards in order to form a sentence. In the initial stages, before a child has learned to handwrite, the teacher will copy the sentence into the child's own sentence book. As he progresses, he will be able to write the sentence for himself. In this way, from the earliest stages, the child is able to compose his own stories and to write and read his own personal book.

It was seen that a published version of Gaelic Breakthrough would be of immense assistance to the schools. So, it was decided to pilot a trial version in a wider selection of schools to discover which words had high frequency of use among children and to decide on a core of about 100 words which could be printed in Gaelic. This done, the project approached Longman Group with a view to obtaining a published version of the folder. Agreement was reached over the publication of a limited number, and the folder entitled 'Na Facail' appeared in Spring 1981.

Once teachers became acquainted with the materials and how to use them, Gaelic Breakthrough proved popular and valuable in the schools. We had only to observe an infant classroom busy with the material to realise the richness of the children's language and the fluency with which it was being expressed. They were completely absorbed as they selected and manipulated words, sought out endings, requested new words, read their story to the teacher and wrote it in their books.

To accompany the Breakthrough folder, the project prepared for printing a Word Book also entitled 'Na Facail'. The book, in alphabetical order, lists all the words in the folder with space available on each page for the child to add his own personal words. It is used by the children at the transitional stage when they are beginning to dispense with their folders as an aid to writing. These books have also proved most useful in the schools.

As mentioned earlier, one of the difficulties encountered by teachers in developing Gaelic writing was the teaching of Gaelic spelling. The team has been seeking ways of tackling this problem and one of the methods used was a trial version of a Gaelic Wordmaker similar to the idea of the 'Breakthrough Wordmaker'. In view of the technically complicated make-up of this material, these wordmakers had all to be hand-made by the team, so that only a limited number could be prepared. These are at present being piloted by selected teachers.

To circumvent the high costs involved in pubishing original Gaelic material with full-colour illustrations, some publishers utilise the method of co-editions where English and Gaelic versions of the same book are published simultaneously. In just such a venture the project team co-operated with Acair in providing Gaelic translations for the first two titles from a series entitled 'Doighean Siubhail air a' Ghaidhealtachd' (Transport in the Highlands). These two titles 'Air an rathad' (Road-ways) and 'Air a' chanal' (Waterways) are suitable for use in the upper primary stages. The Gaelic versions are being used to good effect as reference material on the history of transport.

Similarly, in Spring 1980, one of the team members translated a 4-book series of Bible stories. These were — 'Moire, Mathair Iosa' (Mary, Mother of Jesus), 'Gideon' (Gideon), 'Peadar, An t-Iasgair' (Peter the Fisherman) and 'Rut' (Ruth, the Harvest Girl). In translating the books care was taken to ensure that the language used would be at a level that was simple enough for children to follow. Their appearance in the classroom marked another milestone in Gaelic publication — a most attractive, colourful, fully-illustrated series of Gaelic Bible stories for children. These too were published by Acair.

The project team itself could, naturally, undertake only a limited amount of material production, because of the small size of the team in relation to all the many and varied tasks it was expected to carry out. But it was encouraging to find that other writers were being stimulated to write for children and so provide support for the work. This increase in flow of writing was no doubt due in part to the impact made by the project itself and partly to the fresh outlet for publication provided by Acair and other publishers to satisfy demand from the schools. While much of the material produced was not written by the project team, it was normally written in such a way as to be in line with the aims of the project, consultation having usually taken place between the project and publishers before publication.

A number of books written for children appeared from Acair during this period. 'Rònan agus Brianuilt' written for the upper primary stages provided an imaginative framework through which environmental studies of the local area incorporating history, geography and nature study could be done. The book was serialised as five radio programmes for the BBC Schools Gaelic series 'Co Iad?' and proved most successful in use. Also in the 'Co Iad?' series a unit of ten programmes entitled 'Domhnall MacDhomhnaill MacDhomhnaill' was produced as resource material for the health education area of the curriculum. Written in a most amusing and novel way, this was yet another new area of the curriculum into which Gaelic was introduced. The programmes were later produced in book form. It is used with upper primary pupils. 'MacCurraich agus Cailleach a' Bhrot' (MacCurraich and the Broth Wife) tells of another of the ventures of MacCurraich, the popular character who featured in the 'Cliath' series produced in the first phase. This book has appeal throughout the school range. 'Seinn Seo' (Sing This) is a book/tape of rhymes published for young children. The rhymes were originally written and set to music for the BBC Schools radio series 'Culaidh Mhiogais'. Some of the rhymes were contributed by the project.

In recent months, several books written for adults, of local content on a variety of themes, have appeared from various publishers. While these books were not directed at a primary school audience, they are nevertheless an additional resource for teachers on which to draw for local reference material.

At a less sophisticated level of production the project has continued to be involved in preparing booklets and audio-visual materials to be distributed to schools in published form to supplement what is available from Gaelic publishers. The 'paste-over' books exercise, begun in the first phase, was continued, and six further titles were produced for use in playgroups and infant classes.

From time to time, working parties of teachers met with team members to write stories and poems. These were then usually illustrated by Katherine Barr, an art teacher seconded part-time to the project. They were arranged in booklet form and reproduced by the team for use as trial material in the schools. Among titles produced in this way were 'Aig a' Chladach' (At the Seashore), 'Aig an Abhainn' (At the River), 'Aig an Fhaing' (At the Fank), 'Na Bocsaichean Arain' (The Boxes of Bread), 'A' dol gu Eirisgeidh' (Going to Eriskay), 'Aig a' Chidhe' (At the Quay). The photography skills of team members have been used to advantage in preparing sequences of enlarged black/white prints of local themes such as 'Harvest' and 'Lobster Fishing'. These were used as an aid for stimulating interest in the local environment and developing skills of discussion among young children. A tape/booklet of Gaelic songs and rhymes 'Suilean Dubha' was produced in conjunction with the Community Education Project and distributed to infant classes and playgroups. Also popular with schools and playgroups was a set of 8 illustrated posters produced by the project to accompany the BBC Schools Gaelic Learner series 'Say It In Gaelic'. Not only were these posters used in Western Isles schools and playgroups, they were in popular demand in other Gaelic areas too.

From the outset, the project has been in close touch with developments in BBC Gaelic Broadcasts for schools. Two team members have represented the project on the Gaelic Advisory Panel and recently the project director has taken over as chairman of the panel. In between the annual meetings, the producer maintains close links with the project. This ensures that effective use is made of the programmes in the schools, and vice-versa, that the thinking behind the programmes coincides with the aims of the project. Much excellent Gaelic resource material has been made available to schools in this way. Team members have on occasion provided scripts for the different series.

Over and above material which has been processed as described, the project has collected a wide range of children's work which has been produced around a given theme in the classroom e.g. writing, drawings, slides, tapes, local reference material. This wealth of material represents not only ready evidence of the quality and quantity of the work which has been produced in those classrooms, but also a resource from which further material can be processed. The team have themselves also accumulated a bank of raw resource material such as video-film, slides, tapes, photographs, etc.

The team has always found the production of materials to be an interesting and satisfying task, and this sense of satisfaction may in part be due to the products being more tangible than may be the case in other spheres of the work. There is no doubt but that a considerable amount of time and commitment is required to prepare and see material through all the various stages of production. The team have never been able to devote as much time to it as they would wish, and, strangely, almost feel a sense of unease if they do spend a lot of time on it when conscious of all the other tasks remaining to be done. Fortunately they do not have to shoulder the whole burden in that it is shared with other agencies. In retrospect, it is encouraging to see the progress that has been made, not only in the amount of material which has been produced but also in the more effective use which is being made of it. The use to which it is being put is reflected to some extent in the later chapter on case studies.

5. Case Studies.

Introduction

In broadest terms, the aim of this project is to set up in primary schools in the Western Isles a curriculum which is of direct relevance to the children in these islands — an essential facet of this curriculum being its bilingual nature.

The curriculum being advocated draws on the best in current accepted practice, both in content and in methodology. In content it stresses and seeks to validate, the knowledge which relates to the child's immediate physical and cultural environment. The child is made secure in first-hand experiences of these initially, so as to progress to understand the wider world all the more meaningfully. 'Environmental Studies' is not one subject for the child; it is a comprehensive process by which he utilises his tools of language and cognition to comprehend and represent his world to himself and to others. The value and success of the curriculum is to be gauged by the extent to which it reflects, engages with and recreates the everyday life of the child in his setting.

The method by which this bilingual curriculum is offered to the child, within the aims of this project, also draws on the recognised best in current practice. The teacher is encouraged to enable the child to interact with any topic from a stance of active, interest-based learning. The child is facilitated to have first-hand experience of the work in hand so that all he learns becomes personal knowledge which is then his, to impart to others by the various means at his disposal. Enabling him to develop and hone these very means becomes a central part of the teacher's endeavour i.e. the child's ability to communicate with himself and others through both his languages, verbally and through writing and reading, as well as through drama, art, music and other creative forms.

Such a curriculum aims to socialise the child to have competence and confidence, as well as knowledge of himself and of place, plus the means of knowing how he can continue to learn about these.

The story of how this project introduced such a curriculum into certain primary schools in the Western Isles is one which involves individual teachers. As set out in Chapter 3 the project built up a network of links with teachers in their separate schools. It sought to support their initiatives through discussion, guidance and the provision of certain materials, but it left to the individual teacher's integrity and ingenuity the extent to which the curriculum was implemented in the classroom. The project was set up as a venture which was teacher-centred, as a means of realising a curriculum which was child-centred.

Teachers' accounts of how they fared with this work — their initial understanding of it, and their doubts about it and about their own ability to adopt it, as well as their successes and frustrations — comprise the remainder of this chapter and form the core of the report.

Each setting is different; each teacher is different; each set of children brought to the situation a varied range of interests and proficiency in their two languages, as well as having come from home backgrounds where a variety of attitudes exist towards language and towards schooling.

The case studies included in this report were selected to give as wide a range of situations as possible and with reference to school size, location and proportion of native speakers to learners. The number of studies included is arbitrary but a significant number were included so as to give a general over-view.

The case studies were compiled by the teachers involved. In some cases the teacher wrote the account, in other cases she made a tape recording, and in other cases her account was spoken, and written down by a project fieldworker.

Case Study 1
This is a 2-teacher school with a roll of 27 pupils. I teach P1-4 (13 pupils). Nine are fluent Gaelic speakers, the other 4 have 1 parent who speaks Gaelic. The school is in a crofting community. I have been in the project since it began in 1975.

My choice of theme is usually determined by the interests of the children. It begins through talking, getting the children to talk about their interests and that leads on to further development. At other times the theme may be centred round programmes the children enjoyed on 'Culaidh Mhiogais' — a Gaelic Schools Radio Series. These programmes deal mainly with their own environment, and after listening to them the children are desperate to relate stories concerning their own families, their pets, work on the croft, cattle, sheep, implements, etc. So, the children quite unconsciously guide my choice of topic. My main aims then are to harness their interests and use them to develop discussions which lead on to art work, and then writing their own stories and reading them.

It is very important that children's learning should be based on their environment. They talk spontaneously about any experience they have had. I find the children help one another in discussion. When one child is telling something the other children offer suggestions to help him or her along. In this way the more reluctant child is greatly encouraged. There is far more freedom and a more relaxed atmosphere in the classroom. The children are now never reluctant to approach the teacher for any guidance they may require — I am aware that the children here feel more freedom when expressing themselves in Gaelic; it is more natural for them.

I find also that parents help by supporting the children with information they may require e.g. how croft work was tackled before tractors came to the island. When a child says "thuirt Mamai" (Mammy said) or "thuirt Dadai" (Daddy said) pity help any person who says the information is incorrect. Many an argument this has led to in the classroom — a thing unheard of in pre-project days. This has to be carefully guided in discussion. Children are free to take home Gaelic books and their parents help them to read them or else read them to them.

This environment-based learning does not at all confine them to their own immediate environment. I'll just illustrate the point from one topic — 'Sheep'. Much discussion, drawing, writing and reading is done on the many and varied tasks involving sheep management. All this the children see at first hand and have personal knowledge of:
'Trusadh nan Caorach' (Gathering); 'A' Rusgadh' (Shearing); 'A' Dubadh (Dipping); 'A' Dosadh' (Dosing); 'Caoirich a' Breith' (Lambing); 'Seil nan Caorach' (Sheep Sales).
This naturally leads on to wider research — Where does the wool go? What are the processes? Where is it processed? Where does it eventually finish? — in shops as knitting yarn, blankets, jumpers, etc. Other topics explored in the immediate environment can similarly lead to wider research and understanding of what they may see on TV programmes at home after school hours.

Their main source of learning is from observation and discussion of their environment. Children give a certain amount of information and I channel and guide them to simple books either English or Gaelic that may help to expand knowledge on a topic e.g. — books on birds, birds' eggs, flowers. This is a different to the method used in pre-project days. Then, I used to give the information and tried to find out how much they had understood by direct questioning. The environment was very seldom used then. I also used oral composition using large pictures on the wall. The children gave me sentences about the picture, but they were confined just to what they were seeing. I did not relate the picture to their own experience or background. I have given this up. I though at one time that this helped them with their English but they learn better using the present system. Every subject at that time was in its own compartment. Each subject was taught separately in isolation with the emphasis on the three R's. I don't for one minute want to give the impression that I have done away with the three R's. I now teach all subjects integrated. Gaelic is no longer a subject but is now a teaching medium for various subjects. One must attempt to achieve some sort of balance of topics in the year's plan. I have no problem in selecting and planning themes, the only problem is trying to limit the children's relating of stories! My pupils never tire of talking about themselves, but I know when to draw the line without hurting any feelings. I, myself, seem to be learning along with the children — something new every day.

I work in both English and Gaelic, but Gaelic takes precedence in the infant classroom. I'd say I speak Gaelic to my pupils most of the day. Children now write in Gaelic on Primary 2; a thing unheard of before the project. When I started teaching, emphasis was on teaching children English. I know that most learning was done by rote without understanding.

Discussion now leads to art work, making friezes. I think that if they didn't get the opportunity to draw their stories, there wouldn't be writing at all. Before the project, pictures were first looked at and laid aside. Now they are an important part of learning and development of skills. They talk about their pictures. I record some of this on our tape-recorder. Sometimes we make a slide/tape, using ektragraphic slides. Children love using a camera and photographing the different groups carrying out various activities e.g. measuring the playground, planting potatoes, working at peats. These skills in 'recording' seem to come quite naturally to the children, with a little guidance. Talking is really the basis for the development of all these skills. Children develop confidence to tackle things in this way. Not least in importance is the confidence and motivation to tackle reading and writing. Previously as I have stated most of my teaching was done by giving information and then testing by direct questioning. This led to the tendency of one-word answers in English. I now find that when giving an answer they automatically give it in the form of a short story narrative. Similarly they also ask questions if they want to find anything out.

Before the project, Gaelic skills were not taught until P3 and that first entailed reading. Very little other work was attempted. I used the

'Alasdair agus Mairi' series, reading the book and then filling in blank spaces with the words provided. Now, using 'Breakthrough', children acquire skills of reading and writing at an earlier stage. I had problems with the organisation of the material at the beginning but it has proved to be a blessing in disguise. Now towards the end of P1 and beginning of P2 children are beginning to write simple stories. Children's work is displayed on the walls. At this stage children are very self-centred and are greatly encouraged to see their own work on display. The children from the next room in the P5-7 group come in to see any new pictures whenever they can. Their interest also helps their younger brothers and sisters.

At the end of P2 the children operate very well with the Breakthrough method and on P3 their stories are longer, with the children having a much wider vocabulary. Gradually they are encouraged to make up word books of their own — they have a page or two for each topic. I also use word sheets, displaying words on the topic current at a particular time. I anticipate words the children are likely to use and make up word sheets with them. At P4 stage the children become almost independent of me, using their own word books intelligently.

I can truthfully say that writing and reading in Gaelic have definitely improved. Their English has suffered no loss through learning in both languages. They used to write only one or two sentences in English when given a topic, now they do write more. I would say that by P3-4 they are as advanced in Gaelic as in English, but we would benefit from more Gaelic reading material for the needs of my P2. I think children are happier using their first language. It also makes for a happier relationship between teacher and pupils. The children enjoy their work at this stage and are keen to take Gaelic books home with them as I have stated. Parents co-operate in reading the books with them.

Obviously it benefits the children to know and be literate in two languages. When an English-speaking person approaches the children they are quite capable of conversing with them in English. Actually they have more confidence in themselves to do this than in pre-project times. I myself had fears at first that English would suffer, but I have no fears in that line now.

'Learners' in my class are very anxious to learn the Gaelic language. They wish to join in with the rest of the children. I have proved the Breakthrough to Literacy material works well with 'learners' and soon they are able to write and read Gaelic. They come and ask "How do I say 'such and such' in Gaelic?"

I have a slow learner in P4 who enjoys working in Gaelic whereas in English he seems to become a different person. He is reluctant to attempt English and when I ask him a question in English he invariably answers in Gaelic. He is not shy and talks freely about his family, play, etc. in Gaelic. This is a pupil who would greatly benefit from more published reading material in Gaelic. There has definitely been an improvement as regards Gaelic material, but we are looking for more for the various stages we have. The books are effective and most of them appeal to the children. However, I could do with more for P1 and 2. I have not at the moment many simple enough for my slower pupils on P2.

Generally speaking, I do not take kindly to any changes but my attitude at the beginning was, "I have to try this out so I'd better get on with it". Involvement in the project has taught me a number of things. I enjoy this method of teaching Gaelic. It has certainly taught me to be more aware of my environment and its potential for teaching. I am now quite ready to admit to pupils if there is something I don't know — name of certain flowers, birds, etc. The following morning they may come with the necessary information from their parents. We look up reference books together. Teacher and pupils are on the same level. I find that teachers' meetings are a vitally important part of the work of the project. Ideas are shared and discussed, then tried out in the classroom.

Case Study 2

This is a 3-teacher primary school, the class involved in this study being P4-5. About 40% of the children in this class are Gaelic-speaking with varying degrees of fluency. The area has been subject to an influx of English monolingual incomers over the past few years, and they have had a strong influence on the extent to which Gaelic is used among the children. The school has been involved in the Bilingual Education Project since its inception so I have been involved with it directly since 1976.

I wanted to do an environmental theme during the summer term. I had thought of doing a study of birds in our locality, but being so ignorant about the subject I was afraid to tackle it. In the spring however, at a meeting of a group of mid-primary teachers, the Bilingual Project staff introduced us to what seemed at the time an incomprehensible teaching approach orientated towards the study of the environment. At the meeting we were studying the SCES document 'Towards a Policy for Science in Scottish Primary Schools' and especially Appendix 1 which lists nine concepts which SCES claimed to be basic to environmental science. The teacher group chose 'Birds' as a theme and decided to explore the feasibility of writing all nine concepts into a model plan, whilst being fully aware of the absurdity of incorporating all nine in actual practice. We found this exercise difficult, and at the time I thought it was quite ridiculous and a waste of time. I was later to realise how useful it had been in focusing ideas and teasing out the problems with other teachers. After the meeting I began to think about these ideas more deeply and decided to try the 'Birds' topic with my class, basing my plan on the model drawn up at the meeting.

I did not specify the Gaelic component in the plan at this stage, as it is implicit in all the work we do now, that fluent Gaelic speakers will have ample opportunity to talk, read and write in their own language as well as in English.

My main aim was to lead the children to an understanding of some of the listed concepts and to help them towards a way of expressing these to themselves and to others. To this end, I hoped their powers of observation would be developed, that they would become more aware of the world around them, and that they would gain respect for and sensitivity towards other living creatures in their environment. I hoped their observations would lead them to asking questions such as "Why?" "When?" "How many?"

As the plan was drawn up with the emphasis on concepts, I wrote up activities which we could tackle to get at them. I did not expect to get through very many of these activities, but I found that the highly-structured nature of the plan facilitated the work and I think I can honestly say that all the concepts were tackled in some measure. From the talk, discussion and writing which ensued I could see that the children had a great deal of understanding about some of them e.g. adaptation: birds nests were examined and found to be made up of fluff from hoover-bags and pieces of Kleenex tissue amongst other things. Each time we returned from a trip we would discuss one concept for a long time — days perhaps — examining our evidence from all sources. It helped a lot that they themselves were actively engaged in the subject. They were out looking for themselves. They could see interdependence in action as they watched the birds feed on the ticks that bother the sheep. This had been meaningless to them before. They could better understand things like natural control of insects, worms, slugs. They could see the food chain in action. Their language was enriched by the need to find ways of expressing these concepts, and for those who were bilingual there was a deeper understanding of the concept itself as they sought to articulate meanings in two languages.

I would say from observation of the children through this topic that the Gaelic-speaking children were able to express themselves better in English than their monoglot peers. This was more noticeable with 'less-bright' children. Using Gaelic to express themselves first, and being able to continue the discussion in Gaelic with me, seemed to give them more understanding of the concept itself and to help them to express their meaning in English later on, if that was necessary.

I may mention here that the topic generated tremendous enthusiasm and interest not only among the children but amongst parents, brothers, sisters, grandparents. Ghillies and crofters came forward with much interesting information. Binoculars were provided by many enthusiastic parents and this added to the interest. Bird tables sprouted all over the village, and a few children have been given bird-books as birthday presents by their parents. Children developed skills of observation, listening and unbroken concentration, without which a project of this kind cannot succeed. Listening skills improved considerably. They learned to be very very still and to listen carefully in order to identify bird-song. Discussion skills improved. They had to learn to listen to others and wait their turn. Reference skills became very meaningful. They learned to look up indices and to know which books would yield the required information. Writing developed as they sought to express themselves factually or creatively in both languages. They made charts and records of all they saw and heard, carrying notebooks and pencils with them at all times, in and out of school, and the whole class enrolled as members of the Young Ornithologists Club. They made a collection of poems about birds in both languages and I hope sometime to make a booklet of all the poems they themselves have written.

The method used for this project worked very well for both myself and the children. The plan which I had drawn up and to which I more or less adhered helped me considerably in achieving my aims and in establishing an understanding of the concepts listed. This method was new to me and I was not enamoured of it at the beginning but thanks to the support of the Bilingual Project staff I persevered and would have no hesitation in using it again and recommending it to others. The children were enthralled and would have spent all day on the subject, and although the subject itself has intrinsic appeal I would like to think that careful planning had something to do with their enthusiasm. I have been learning with the children and it has been a worthwhile experience for all concerned.

Case Study 3
This is a 2-teacher primary department attached to a secondary school. There have always been some non-Gaelic speaking children in each class since I began teaching here. Nevertheless, before the Bilingual Education Project began, and also during the early years of the project, the majority of children were fluent Gaelic speakers. Over the years, there has, for various reasons, been a gradual change so that, in 1981, Primaries 1-2 (21 pupils) is made up of 6 fluent Gaelic speakers (with both parents speaking Gaelic) 5 learners (with neither parent having any knowledge of Gaelic) and 10 other learners with one parent able to speak Gaelic. Some years ago one could depend on most of the new entrants being fluent

Gaelic speakers, and that once they had mastered the basics of reading in Gaelic they could progress rapidly because they understood so well what they were reading. This is no longer the case.

Occasionally there are learners whose parents are not interested in whether the children have Gaelic or not, but in most cases, expecially where one parent is a Gaelic speaker, they are very anxious that their children should have Gaelic. There are other cases where Gaelic has skipped a generation (the children were brought up on the mainland and have returned as adults to work here), and parents desire to let their children have this skill of which they themselves were deprived. In one such case a parent of some of my pupils now goes to evening classes to learn Gaelic in order to be a help to the children at home.

Obviously teachers have to adapt to changes of circumstances in the classroom. Where learners are in the majority, the methods of teaching Gaelic have to change and adapt to the needs of the pupils. In days gone by there were no beginners' books in Gaelic, no alphabet books, no books with simple captions, no graded infant readers such as one finds in English, and although teachers would have welcomed them, their lack was not felt as keenly as it is now, with Gaelic being taught to most pupils here as a second language.

In the absence of suitable materials for teaching Gaelic to young learners, teachers with the assistance of the Bilingual Project have had to experiment with methods of presenting material in interesting and stimulating ways to learners and to try to fill the gap which exists between present learners' needs and the books which are becoming available through the project. Sometimes the teachers met and devoted afternoons to writing simple stories, rhymes or poems, which were later illustrated, duplicated and issued to teachers. If there were 6 teachers in the group and each one produced 2 pieces of writing that meant that finally each teacher would receive 12 little stories or poems to ease the dearth of Gaelic materials in her classroom.

I have for some years been trying out and working with materials for Gaelic teaching based on the 'Breakthrough to Literacy' programme which is available in English, and it was with great pleasure that I heard that a Gaelic version of the pupils sentence maker was being made available through the Bilingual Project. The children are now using it to good effect and I feel its value will be further enhanced by a reading scheme for infants built round the words contained in the folder and the ideas which stem from their use by children.

The Bilingual Project has always advocated that the basis of language work should be a topic familiar to the children, through which they can develop skills of listening, talking, reading, writing etc. At the present time our topic is 'Ag Iasgach' (Fishing) and the children have been motivated, by photographs given by the Bilingual Project, to relate their own experiences or knowledge of boats, fishing, collecting shellfish, etc. Art work has been centred on this theme and also music. We use the same material and topic for English language development, and it was in a written story by Primary 3 that it was noted that although they were familiar with words like 'lighthouse' and 'net' they were not familiar with their function. One child wrote — "Fishermen make for a lighthouse when there is a storm." Therefore explorations of topics such as this serve many purposes, they are vehicles for the use, development and extension of language both in Gaelic and English and also serve to extend children's knowledge and conceptual development.

My method of teaching Gaelic to 'learners' in P1 is to let them have ample opportunity of listening and trying to understand simple phrases used in the everyday classroom routine e.g. 'Duin an doras' (Close the door), 'Tog an leabhar' (Pick up the book), 'Dean dealbh bàta' (Draw a boat). When they have a fair knowledge of such phrases I try to tell simple stories with lots of repetition when the children can join in the chorus. I also use the two cassette tapes 'Sùilean Dubha' and 'Seinn Seo' which have simple songs to stimulate further participation and enjoyment of the language. Thus by listening to, repeating and acting out situations which crop up in the daily routine the children will be familiar with the sound of Gaelic and the meaning of everyday words.

By the time children are on P2 they usually have sufficient knowledge to start using the 'Breakthrough' folders already mentioned to make sentences, initially with the help of the teacher and eventually on their own. By P3 they are able to use all the words in the 'Breakthrough' folder and thus be able to become independent of their folders and use instead their own personal dictionary of Gaelic words which will be added to continually as they tackle various themes throughout the year.

The children enjoy their Gaelic work and the work seems to be effective insofar as the teacher is able to be with the children, but in a busy composite classroom the teacher's personal attention is taken up with a great variety of difficult work so that the time spent on direct pupil/teacher interaction is limited to an extent. I feel that a great deal of back-up material is needed to help such teachers even if such material only serves to reinforce what the teacher has been trying to teach. P3 especially could engage in more work on their own if there was a greater variety of books and materials geared to their needs.

Case Study 4

This study was undertaken with P3/4 in a 5-teacher school. The large majority of children are fluent Gaelic speakers, there being only one learner in the class at present. I have been in the BEP for two years, having previously taught in city and town schools.

The children in this class are drawn from an area in the north of the island from which, in the early autumn of each year, a number of men go to spend three weeks on the island of Sulasgeir. Hundreds of young gannets are killed and brought home and local people at home and abroad eagerly await the landing of this delicacy. The gannet has been a staple food here for many generations and the trip to Sulasgeir is a highlight in the local calendar. Therefore, at this time of the year, the trip to Sulasgeir is the major talking point in the district and the children become very excited about it.

The topic arose quite naturally from the children's interest and conversation at this time. They talked such a lot about it that I decided to make a tape of their conversation, just to assess the extent of their interest and knowledge, and to give me a starting point on which to build a topic plan. The tape showed me that they were intensely interested but only vaguely knowledgeable, so I began to draw up a plan on which the term's work could be based. I used Sulasgeir as a focal point and attempted to integrate as many subjects as possible according to the children's understanding and ability at this stage.

Fortunately at this time, there is only one child who is not a totally fluent Gaelic speaker, so Gaelic is the natural medium for a lot of work. The children feel very much at home in the Gaelic language, especially on a topic such as this which is widely discussed at home. The tape was very enlightening on this point.

After an initial question or two by me to get them going I was able to withdraw almost completely. They argued quite a bit and brought the discussion forward in this way. It was as if they drew language and information out of one another. If the English speaker happened to be present they tended to begin by translating and then continue in English. If I were taking part in the discussion I found that if they spoke in English, I translated their remarks into Gaelic. I had never been aware of doing this, so it was very interesting.

To stimulate their interest further at this point I asked one of the teachers in the secondary department, who belongs to the area, to come and talk to them about the historical aspect of the topic and to answer the many questions which had arisen since we started our discussions. His visit was a great success. It surprised us both that it gave the children a great sense of importance that a 'Secondary Teacher' had spoken to them. They boasted about it to other classes and talked a lot about what he had said. I suppose it shows how remote 'the secondary' feels to these children and that barriers exist of which we may be unaware. Anyway this particular teacher now visits the class regularly and has helped a lot to give them a deeper insight into the topic. The discussions he has had with them has enriched their vocabulary and language. This is evident in our subsequent discussions. He showed them a film taken thirty years ago and they were able to compare the type of boats and the methods used then to the sophisticated means at their disposal now.

Another person who came to talk to them was the school janitor, who has been one of the gannet-hunters for many years. He was able to give us a detailed picture of conditions on the island; how it felt to sleep in a bothy on a lonely rock in the Atlantic; the cries of thousands of seabirds, etc. He explained the meaning of the word Sulasgeir. Again they gained a sense of importance from having the janitor talk to them about his experiences. A lot of talk and writing in both languages, drawing and model-making followed these visits. It seemed to 'come alive' for them, having had these experiences shared. We also had a lot of help from the local Historical Society who gave us old photographs, newspaper cuttings and articles on loan.

Running parallel with these visits was the environmental component of the plan which took the children out of the classroom to make close observations in the immediate vicinity of the school and slightly further afield. The janitor spoke to them about the bird-life on the island and the flora and fauna, or lack of it. This raised questions in their minds and they studied plants and flowers near the school and on the machair and asked why such flowers grew there but not on the island. The most exciting trip outside was when we went to look at the sea in an angry mood on a really windy day. Another day we went to observe it in a quiet mood. We built up word-banks and phrase-banks to help them describe these scenes in both languages. They talked it through and produced a lot of good writing. I feel sure now that the best written work comes through the children experiencing and feeling for themselves, and this is dependent on what the teacher is prepared to put into it. There must be a lot of talk, discussion, visual aids, word-banks, help with phrasing, etc. before good writing can be expected.

A lot of the learning the children have done through this particular topic has been through the Gaelic language, simply because it was the natural language of this topic. This does not mean that the English language was neglected. They are exposed to English at all times and particularly through the written word. All written reference material is in English and although these children are fluent Gaelic speakers and a lot of their understanding of concepts comes about through the medium of Gaelic, they are also fluent English speakers and have the skill of expressing meanings in both languages. Because the children have this skill, the teacher may choose to shift the balance from time to time as she sees fit, as long as she ensures that development in both languages has been maintained throughout the year. I do not consciously compartmentalise either language. We seem to use the one which comes naturally at the time.

The striking thing about this particular topic has been that, as it developed, my own role became increasingly passive as the children work for stretches of time on their own. They have gained a great sense of confidence and independence and that is very satisfying.

The bilingual mode of teaching was completely new to me when I started at this school. In fact it was like a culture shock to hear children addressing me in Gaelic, as this was a completely new experience. I was very nervous about this at first and very aware of my own limitations, but I find I am learning with the children and feel more confident about this mode. The teachers' meetings have helped me a lot also. I always feel stimulated and refreshed having thrashed out ideas and exchanged problems with other teachers. I would like to have a lot more of these meetings.

Case Study 5

This school is a 2-teacher primary with children drawn from the surrounding villages. Most of the children in the school are Gaelic-speaking, there being only 1 child in this P5, 6, 7 class who is not a fluent speaker. The school became involved in the Bilingual Education Project at the beginning of its second phase and this involvement has guided us towards tackling the curriculum in new ways which we would not have thought possible before.

I selected this particular theme at this time because this year we have a boy who suffers from muscular dystrophy so we had to study an area near the school, but as we had done a shore study before, I wanted to do something different that would stimulate them from the start. I was a bit stuck for a topic and it was decided to make a study of animal homes on the shore and on the machair. I felt this would encourage them to observe different aspects of their own environment and that they might study homes such as nests, rabbits burrows, creatures in shells, creatures with no homes etc in some detail. I hoped this would lead them to an awareness of some of the concepts discussed in the SCES paper such as adaptation, dependence-interdependence, comparison, location particularly, and also provide an opportunity to learn new skills such as close observation and recording, and reinforce the skills of reference, discussion and different types of writing. Implicit in all this of course was that the children who brought the skill of the Gaelic language to the theme would have an opportunity to extend and develop that language, that they would learn new vocabulary pertaining to the subject being studied and that their understanding of the concepts before us would be enriched by their ability to express their ideas in 2 languages. This approach to the

Gaelic language is quite different in that it is now used to express ideas and concepts which previously would have been confined to English.

There was a lot of discussion with the children to start with. The fluent speakers undertake all discussion in Gaelic. As we had only 3 non-Gaelic speakers during this term and they had been very keen learners, they were able to chip in and made themselves understood in whichever language they chose. I involved everybody from the start and if the non-Gaelic speakers had difficulty, I would translate as I went along or one of the children would translate. Sometimes the learners made a valiant effort to take part in the discussion in Gaelic, but this requires a great deal of time. They had been following the Gaelic Learners BBC Schools programme 'Toiseach Toiseachaidh' which helped them a lot.

Immediately after this they started to look around — to and from school, at playtimes etc and very soon someone reported an oyster-catcher's nest near the shore. Naturally we all went to see it, and as the bird was not on the nest we were able to examine the eggs and take a photograph of them. The nest was just a hollow in the sand. They were very excited about it, so a great variety of nests were reported in the next few days. During further visits to the beach we were able to photograph the nests of a herring gull, a tern and a black-headed gull. Some of the eggs were just about to hatch and later they came back and photographed the young chicks. All this activity stimulated a keen interest in birds. Reference books were much in demand and they kept records of what they saw each day.

But I wanted to move them on to look at other animals and creatures, so we discussed this and they started further observations. Soon they were studying shells, hermit crabs, worm-casts, insect homes round the school etc. They seemed to be either delving under stones or into reference books all the time. The interesting thing from the language point of view here was that, since most of the discussion of the topic was in Gaelic, when they extracted an interesting bit of information from an English reference book, they discussed it with me in Gaelic. I noticed that their oral proficiency in both languages improved, because they discussed everything with me in Gaelic and with their non-Gaelic speaking peers in English. Hence there was an extension and an enrichment of their vocabulary in both languages.

About this time the bad weather limited their activity outside so I suggested they might look at people's homes. They immediately began to look at houses in the locality, to note the differences, compare old with new etc. Parents were very helpful at this point, giving information about types of homes they could remember. As they searched through reference books for more information, they began to comment on types of homes in other lands. They became so interested in this aspect of the topic that there was no holding them back, and although I was keen to confine the study to the local area, I did not wish to spurn their enthusiasm. They organised themselves into groups and decided between themselves which country or part of the world they wished to study. Modelling became the order of the day, and wigwams, igloos, mud huts, thatched cottages and multi-storeys began to sprout. They brought in cuttings from newspapers e.g. the collapse of a building in Glasgow and began to be involved with the people who lived in 'their' homes.

In this way the geographical aspect was well catered for and historical studies arose from such questions as "When were castle built and why?" "What about monasteries?" I felt rather worried for a time as the topic had taken off in a direction which I never originally intended. But the children themselves were so enthusiastic that I could not have stopped them or a lot would have been lost.

Undoubtedly their oral proficiency in both languages improved as I have already described. Their reading was widened to such an extent, that I now realise that it is through this experiential approach that real learning takes place. Since we started learning to 'look' they have learned so much and I have been learning with them. We have moved from abstract book learning to learning from handling, feeling, experiencing, and this has made the subsequent book learning more meaningful. I think that is one thing this particular theme has shown. By looking at homes at many levels of life in their own environment, they sought out information from books because they wanted to know, not because they were told to do so by someone else. And when it came to written work, the same was true. They wanted to record their discoveries at each stage, and with so much practice, became equally fluent in Gaelic and English. Children who formerly used a lot of English words now find a Gaelic word to express the idea.

As to the realisation of my initial aims, I think we have catered for the main ones in some way. But one striking feature has been the enthusiasm with which the children have tackled this, and I think it may be because I wasn't pushing them towards any aspect in particular but allowing the study to develop naturally, and the responsibility being on themselves to develop it. This does not mean that we would work like this all the time. The year's work has to be structured and planned and a balance maintained.

I must also point out that this mode of working was completely new to me as a teacher. Before our school was involved in the Bilingual Project, I used to think it wasn't right to go outside and 'waste time'. We used to go for walks on the shore but I did not regard this as having any educational value. I kept thinking of what we 'should' be doing in the classroom.

Now I realise how much we have all gained from this study and from other studies we have undertaken in this way, and the gains for the skills of discussion, reading, and writing are self-evident from the level which these skills have now attained in both languages.

Case Study 6

After spending some years in fairly deprived city areas I became interested in the slow learner. I gained a diploma in Special Education in 1976, after which I taught in special school till I transferred to a project school in the Western Isles in 1978. This particular school is in a semi-crofting area with part council housing. It is a 2-teacher school. There is a fair proportion of incomers to the area who do not speak Gaelic so that this school has a fairly large percentage of Gaelic-learner children. Over a year ago I transferred from teaching of upper primary to lower primary so that I now teach primaries 1-4.

I found that the Bilingual Education Project provided me with welcome help in adjusting from my teaching post in a special school in the city to teaching of bilingual upper primary children in the Western Isles. The resource centre at Claddach Kirkibost also proved to have excellent reference books and material which I could borrow for project work as necessary. The method of teaching, i.e. through environmental studies at first hand experience, was fairly new to me, at least to the extent to which the method is employed in Bilingual Project schools. I realise, however, that taking the children out of doors proves beneficial and stimulating, providing far better quality of language work in both Gaelic and English.

Given that a third of my class are Learners I felt the need to help these children with the Gaelic language. My reasons for desiring that Learner children eventually become fluent in Gaelic are as follows:
1) The ability to speak/understand/be literate in Gaelic would be an advantage to learners in that there would then be no barriers of communication between them and native speakers.
2) It would be an advantage in the community in that there would be better communication between learners and Gaelic speaking adults and especially old people of the community.
3) There is the added all-round enrichment which goes with the know-ledge of a second language.

I felt that my first step should be to teach oral Gaelic — simple words, phrases and sentences taught in an enjoyable context. My method of teaching is as follows:

I tell a story in Gaelic discussing it with the children as I go along. Discussion takes place in Gaelic and English as is necessary for all children to understand the story. After that we go through the story again, the children as a whole group (i.e. P1-4, fluent and learners together) miming parts of the story as I tell it e.g. they mime the old man in the story, or the child in the story . . . doing that character's various actions throughout the story.

Using the same story again, I get a fluent speaker to tell the story in my place and the rest of the class mime parts of the story as before. Then we progress to the children as a whole group saying Gaelic phrases or sentences with rhythm e.g.
"Chaneil fhios aig duine air thalamh,
Gur e mise Ruairidh Robach."
or
"Di-luain, Di-mairt, Di-ciadain,
Bhàsaich bodach an t-siabain."
Musical instruments are sometimes used at this point. By repetition of sentences in an enjoyable context and relaxed atmosphere, sentences patterns are being established in the learner children's minds.

One has to treat learner children in a very sensitive manner in order to ensure that one does not destroy their self-confidence i.e. they must not be afraid to attempt words/sentences even if they are not altogether correctly spoken. When children are together in a group, learners are less inhibited and actually gain confidence through the support of the fluent speakers in the group, to whom they look for help.

My own role is not a very dominant one; in fact I try to get them to the stage where they are so engrossed in the story that they forget my presence, although in a subtle way I am still directing the procedure. When children see me sitting/kneeling on the floor with them, or miming/acting a story with them, they feel that I am no longer just instructing, that I am with them as one of them. It is very important to ensure that any barriers which may exist between us are broken down and that the classroom atmosphere is relaxed and free.

Children ask to repeat stories which we have already done. This shows enjoyment on the part of the children. They take things to school which relate to the stories e.g. old photographs, stories. They readily take any materials which may be necessary for this type of work e.g. for the making of puppets.

I inform parents who come to the classroom of my work. Parents are free to come and talk to me at any time about the children's work but some come more readily than others. One parent actually made all the puppets for a puppet show once.

There is evidence that Gaelic skills learnt orally carry over into the children's written Gaelic work. They have a better understanding of the basics of Gaelic — this comes through in their written work. They also write with more confidence. They are not inhibited to come to me for help at any time with Gaelic words, oral or written, which they do not understand or wish to use. The amount of time which I devote to oral work of this kind with learners is approximately half an hour per day. It varies however, in that some days we don't do any, other days we do more than the half-hour.

Case Study 7
This is a 3-teacher school in which I have been teaching for over 2 years, having come from a city school. In my first year in this school I taught the infant classes, so this is my first year with this P4-5 class, and my first experience of bilingual education.

My main aim in setting up this study was to attempt to bring meaning to a landmark in the children's environment — the Whalebone Arch at Bragar. The story lends itself to the Gaelic language and I hoped the study would leave them with very worthwhile impressions and feelings, together with an idea of the permanence of things in their environment, so that they identify in some measure with the people who lived here at the time when the story took place. Further objectives were to integrate as many subjects as possible in the study and to use the medium of Gaelic as well as English for all learning throughout the study.

I began planning during the summer holidays. I went to visit someone who lived very near the site and who knew the shores and rocks very well. He took me round the coast and identified all the points, reefs, and bays connected with the story. I realised then that it would be possible to take a class of children there, and that was a very exciting prospect, as it would have been impossible for them to imagine the scene without visiting the site. I decided that the best thing to do would be to set up a 'Whale trail' and follow the story as it happened.

I knew a version of the story had been published in 'Gairm' (a Gaelic magazine) some time ago. I realised this version was much too difficult for the children to read having been written for adults. The author was a friend of mine so I asked her if she could write a version suitable for 8-9 year olds. She was delighted and let me have the story very soon. I broke it up into 6 sections, these being the natural breaks and I had these typed and photocopied as reading material. I started collecting information, old photographs, anything to do with whales in general, that whale in particular. People got to hear of my interest and offered photographs, maps etc. By the beginning of the autumn term, I was totally enthusiastic and ready to do. The first section of the topic was 'Whales in general'. This part would be mainly in English, because all the reference books and materials for this part were in English. The children became very interested at the very outset. I think this is a subject which has an instant appeal to children and since many reference books were available they soon became very enthusiastic. They brought in more reference books themselves. We wrote to the National Museum, Edinburgh, children brought in a whales tooth, baleen etc. At this time also there was a series of TV programmes on whales — 'Wildlife on One' did 'The Humpback Whale'. John Craven did 'Greenpeace'. It was all go. Also at this time, the Bilingual Project arranged a visit by members of the crew of the 'Quattro Venti' who were doing research into whales and dolphins round the British Coast and were in Stornoway for a day or two. This was a most enjoyable experience for the children, giving them the feeling that they were taking part in something which interested adults throughout the world. I feel they got a lot more than just information out of that visit, and contact has been maintained with these people since they returned to various parts of the world.

Written work developed astonishingly from these experiences and resources. At this stage written work was mainly in English. We were now ready for the next stage — preparation for the outing. We read the first reading extract and they became pre-occupied with the size of the whale. They went into the playground to measure the actual size and discovered that it wouldn't fit into the playground. This was very exciting.

They had to go out to the road. Amazed that any living thing could be that big. Ample opportunity for mathematical part of the topic here and this was done — measurement, scale, comparison of sizes, weight etc. The concepts became meaningful to them as they tackled them in relation to this massive creature. Mapping was begun, a map of the local area drawn up showing the route we were to take on the outing. Again the purpose made the exercise meaningful. The Gaelic language now became the natural language of the topic. As they read extracts and I provided further descriptions I could sometimes feel a silence in the room as they appeared to listen to the sounds of words. I didn't expect them to fully understand the language I was using at this point but they seemed to enjoy it and I would find certain words and phrases being used in their discussion and writing which they certainly did not know before. This was good and I intended to continue in this way.

The story begins at 'Geodha na Muic' (The Cave of the Whale) and now they knew how to get there, and they knew the first part of the story. We went on a Saturday — a beautiful day — and the children acted as guides to the driver, following the maps which they had made. At Geodha na Muic we tried to re-live the scene as villagers gathered in 1920 to see the whale. I used this opportunity to use as many descriptive words as I could think of, the children supplied phrases they knew to describe the sea. Imagined the danger involved in towing the great creature to the landing place round the point. As we made our way round to the Sgeir

Mhaol (Blunt Rock), I told them that part of the story. We walked up the hill where the jawbone had been dragged and they could see the dangers and difficulties, as they imagined the horses pulling the huge sledge and the villages pushing it. Then on to the arch, which by now really meant something and where I told them the end of the story — apart from one dramatic incident which I decided to keep till later; they had had enough excitement for one day.

After this experience they were alive with enthusiasm about every aspect of the topic. We still had to cover a number of the reading extracts and those were attacked with vigour and enjoyment. By this time their vocabulary, in both languages, had extended considerably and they each had their word and phrase books to help them to express their thoughts and feelings in writing. To begin with a lot of their writing had been descriptive, now they were producing more creative, expressive material. I was so inundated with Gaelic writing at this time that I felt I couldn't cope. They collected and composed poems and songs about the sea in both languages, they listened to tapes of songs such as 'An Ataireachd Ard', they did finger-painting, paintings, large friezes, photograph albums, tapes, and finally mounted a display of all this work in the P6 room, where parents were able to come and browse around and study the children's work.

I found this topic absolutely excellent as an exercise to bring meaning to something which was part of the children's environment, which was my main aim. But it was much more than that. It provided opportunities for children to experience and discover and feel for themselves and in this way to clarify meanings and express them in new ways.

I am convinced there is no better method that I know of and I wouldn't think of teaching any other way. The enthusiasm, excitement and interest was maintained right through, and the gains for their oral, reading and writing skills have been considerable. Their aesthetic awareness has been heightened, and they feel confident in expressing themselves not only through language but through music, art and drama. I now hope this kind of curiosity and interest, having been aroused so much through this topic will become part of their approach to many things.

Case Study 8
This is a two-teacher primary school situated in a sparsely populated crofting area. The school has a roll of 27 pupils, and I teach a P5/6/7 class of 14 pupils. All the children are fluent Gaelic speakers with the exception of four whose first language was English. Those four have local parents apart from two of the mothers. The four children spent their early years in Lowland Scotland.

My first teaching years were spent in a Glasgow school but I returned to the islands a long time ago. This school has been in the project since it started in 1976 but my class did not participate till the second year.

The theme completed before the October holiday this year was begun shortly after Easter. Since we had the previous summer undertaken a study of the peat bogs and heath close to the school, I thought it would be appropriate to make a study of the machair this year, especially as the children had shown such a keen interest.

My aims were:

a) to give the children opportunities to apply, in practical situations, skills they had already learned e.g. pie charts, graphs and probability;

b) to learn new skills using horizontal and vertical measurements to draw the profile of the pit;

c) to give further practice in the language arts e.g. discussion, writing, both factual and imaginative, and reading interpretation.

In addition the children would see for themselves the differences between the two areas and the changes that occurred in one of the areas from summer to autumn. They would also observe how man used the natural resources of each area.

As well as identifying the plants and noticing similarities and differences between the two areas, exercises were carried out applying what they had previously learned in the classroom about probability, to find which plants were rare, dominant, frequent etc in areas chosen at random. We had discussions and written work in both Gaelic and English on the crops produced, work done, and fertilisers used. At a later stage the older children attempted to make a profile of an old sandpit while the younger ones investigated the plants growing in the bottom of the pit. In autumn we looked for changes in the area we had studied in the summer and concentrated on seeds and their dispersal. The art teacher helped the children to make designs using plant shapes and numerous shades of green. This was most interesting and successful. 'Island of Horses' by Eilis Dillon was the fiction book chosen to accompany the theme, but we did not begin to read it until August, having had difficulty in locating copies. It is a story set in the Aran Islands and is about two teenage boys who explore an uninhabited island used by dishonest horse dealers. Study of the characters and language used gave us many ideas and helped with discussion and writing in both Gaelic and English.

I had the theme planned out beforehand, but I found that the Summer Term was too short for what I had set out to do, the weather unusually wet, and the site rather far away, so the plan was changed a little to suit the Autumn Term.

When forward planning was first suggested, it seemed a formidable task, as we were confronted with ideas and suggestions for schemes for the whole seven years of primary school. However, I discovered that if one has a general idea of what would be realistic to attempt in a year and concentrate on one term at a time, it is not too taxing. I try to keep a fair balance of subjects throughout the year, incorporating Language Arts, Geography, History, and Natural History. Otherwise there might be the danger that one would concentrate too much on certain skills and concepts and neglect others. I also generally try to fit in a relevant work of fiction. Formerly, I used to choose the theme and just get started. As the weeks progressed, new ideas would occur, but sometimes one felt that work was done because it related to the theme and not because it ensured progress for the pupils. I am not entirely satisfied with my present efforts but I hope that with experience they will improve.

As I mentioned earlier, we work in both languages, but I find that certain aspects of my theme are better done in Gaelic. Much of the discussion is done in Gaelic but either language is acceptable. I cannot imagine any situation in this school at least, where a local topic would benefit from being discussed solely in English. We did not experience difficulties with spoken language since we change from one to the other constantly anyway, but they do have a wider vocabulary in their mother tongue. I feel discussion is valuable since it encourages children to ask questions, to listen to what others have to say, and to see things from different angles so that they have a better understanding of it by the end of the discussion. It enables the teacher to see if the children can fully understand the concept.

In writing Gaelic, we initially had great difficulties, but these are now getting less. We use various methods to improve the writing. By following advice from the BEP fieldworkers and other teachers I began using 'Breakthrough to Literacy' for classes 4 and 5. The class was at the time reading 'Charlotte's Web' by E.B. White, a story about a spider, so our writing focussed on this book. Using 'Breakthrough' as an aid, the class made great progress. 'Breakthrough' is used in the infant room now and I don't use it at all, but I have been making enquiries about the 'Wordmaker'. The children themselves now begin to build up a word book of words they have already used. Any new words they ask for, I write on the blackboard. I later transfer these to sheets of sugar paper which I pin to the wall and leave for reference. These are arranged alphabetically and additional words are added as children ask for them. Two of the children are likely to come for help in expressing their ideas in Gaelic.

Different kinds of writing are attempted. For example in creative writing they wrote about what was discovered, buried and preserved in the bog, how the horses came to the deserted island etc. Where their vocabulary is limited a lot of enrichment has to be done. BBC Schools Gaelic radio programmes have been used to help their creative writing e.g. one in which they were encouraged to look for pictures in the clouds, and others in which feelings such as envy were investigated. Factual writing was done on experiments we had carried out and what our findings were. They write alternately in English and Gaelic. I have stopped teaching formal grammar, spelling and repetitive English exercises. These are now based on children's needs as shown in their written work. They keep lists of their own spelling mistakes and errors are corrected as they occur. The kind of writing the children do now is different in that they are composing their own stories or writing them from their own experiences, while formerly they copied sentences from a book filling in blanks, or else they dealt with questions which could be answered by copying from the text. I did not use to teach writing in the way I do now, because I thought children should be proficient readers before they began to write. Obviously we are not complacent about the achievements in writing, but I think we are progressing.

It is difficult to say whether present day children are more fluent readers, but now they generally read at first sight, while formerly children had a class reader and lessons were prepared and read orally several times. We do not now use a Gaelic reading book as in the past, but they have access to more Gaelic books as well as English. I would hesitate to say that they are as advanced in Gaelic reading as in English because there is not the same wealth of material in Gaelic. What is available is more attractive and the increased availability of it has widened their reading experience. We can now afford to be more discriminating as the amount of material increases. We ourselves also prepare Gaelic material in the classroom, relating to the themes we are studying.

I feel it is important that children's learning should begin with their own experiences. This was brought home to me first when we were reading 'The Boy with the Bronze Axe' by Kathleen Fidler. We were able to visit a wheelhouse and a barp and this gave deeper meaning to what they had been reading about in the book. I am sure that our study of the local river helped the children to understand more fully the TV programmes they later saw of the River Tay. It must have also helped when they read part of 'Salar the Salmon' by Henry Williamson and made a study of the fish farm. On another occasion we happened to be studying the peat bog when the threat of 11% increase in price of electricity in diesel areas bothered us all. Interest in peat and other types of fuel was evident and many of the contributions to our discussion had been voiced at home. So in fact these direct experiences give an added meaning to what they read or see on television. It brings reality to the learning. Misconceptions about size, distances, can be corrected and I have discovered that teachers can have these as well as children. Though one uses the local environment as a starting point the learning is not all confined to it. All children benefit from this approach and those below average attainment in the classroom are given more incentive to learn. By building on the child's experience and previous knowledge children approach the work with enthusiasm and confidence.

We use a variety of methods of recording our experiences. The tape-recorder has been used to interview people like the manager of the fish farm, and also to record what the children want to say about the ektagraphic slides they produce periodically. We were lucky in having an Art teacher who helped the children with camera work. They produced good photographs of the river study, and at a later date on the hill. The river photographs were used to produce a little booklet 'An Abhainn' (The River) where children wrote paragraphs about the waterfall, the marsh marigolds, or whatever the photograph portrayed. In art work, figures in wire and papier-mache have been made and dressed. We have also experimented a little with drama, preparing and tape-recording a 'radio' play about life 'air an airigh' (on the shieling).

We sometimes experience difficulty locating appropriate books for our themes of study. The Bilingual Project advisers are very helpful by looking out suitable books and the library boxes are generally good if one can get the one required. Nevertheless more books in Gaelic are needed. Books such as 'Calum Cille' (St Columba) and 'Na Lochlannaich' (The Vikings) are useful reference books. Some more children's books in Gaelic on Island subjects such as the History of the Western Isles, Folk Tales, and the research made by archaeologists locally would be welcome.

Parents, to begin with, were doubtful about the validity of teaching through Gaelic. They felt that the children would not be able to cope with life in the Secondary School if they did not learn in English from the first primary class upward. Neither we nor the Project Team took any formal steps to explain the changes in method to the parents but I think that any parent who takes an interest in the child's education can see there have been many changes in recent years (VRQ dropped, Comprehensive Education etc). Most of them feel that Gaelic speakers are getting a better deal now. They have always approved of Gaelic and they know that their children are more fluent in English than was ever the case before. Their fears like ours were groundless. They show an interest in the children's work, offering plant cuttings, bulbs, oyster shells, cuttings from papers and magazines etc.

Learning through Gaelic has no detrimental effect on the children's learning of English. The children are generally able to apply a skill learned through either language to work done through the other, though it can be noted that at present they are more skilful in using English books of reference, reading and writing in English, while discussion, expression of feeling, relating news and interviewing are better when done in Gaelic. I do not attempt to teach much formal maths in Gaelic since I look on mathematical language as something they have to become familiar with and easy to use. This approach also needs to be carefully planned from their early years so that children can steadily build up expertise. I am glad that all the children had some knowledge of Gaelic coming to my class. The less fluent are able to join the others, although they do need more assistance in expressing their thoughts.

I thought that I would never be able to cope with the work of the project, but now I find that I enjoy learning with the children. I find the change in teaching methods refreshing. To begin with I was reluctant to make what appeared to be a very drastic change, but I was realistic enough to know that it was impossible to teach Gaelic speaking children solely through English. The biggest hurdle where I was concerned was the approach advocated for mapping, but whatever the theme chosen in the first year, I would probably have experienced difficulty in adapting to it. Contact with the Bilingual Project team and with other teachers is now appreciated much more than it was at the beginning. Seeing the efforts of other teachers awakens new enthusiasm and their ideas and plans spur one on to further work. I am becoming more confident though I certainly do not feel I know it all. I must admit to casting envious glances at some of the work produced by other teachers especially that of investigations of the local environment. We know what is expected of us now and we get more help in achieving it. I also feel the content of the curriculum has been improved. Though we had always spoken in Gaelic to each other, one sometimes felt that in doing so one lessened their chances of doing well in the Verbal Reading Test at 11 and 12. Now that Gaelic has official approval, I use it wherever possible, since I certainly consider it an asset for a person to be bilingual.

Since the new approach is more interesting and stimulating for the teachers, these feelings are also conveyed to the children. They are also more confident. They have a friendly attitude to the teacher and look upon her as the leader of a team rather than someone to be feared. They are more motivated to work than formerly. They become absorbed in the subject as they progress. They appreciate books and learn good reading habits as their knowledge increases, be that gained from books or personal experiences. The quality of the work improves as a result.

Case study 9
I teach P1-4 in this 2-teacher school. Over the last few years a large number of English monolingual children have come into this area and

133

this year's intake has shown a sharp decline in the number of fluent Gaelic speaking children. This new situation forces me to set up strategies for work with learners, as I feel I am not able to do so much work in Gaelic as I have been accustomed to doing since the advent of the Bilingual Education Project. I have been in the BEP for 6 years.

At the beginning of this session, the headteacher and I decided that we would attempt a 'whole-school' topic based on occupations in the immediate locality. At my own stage (P1-4) it had to be something very simple and based on something very near to the experience of P1 children who had just entered school. We discussed the possibilities at length and I finally decided that 'People who help us' would be ideal at this stage as people such as the local postman, nurse, doctor, minister were well known to all children. There would thus be an opportunity for the children's attention to be focused on the services provided by these people, the concept of dependence/interdependence would be encountered, and perhaps those people would gain an insight and a greater understanding of how children learn. I especially hoped that children would look more closely at certain aspects of their own environment and be able to to define them in their own language. Since I have a large number of children in my class who are not fluent Gaelic speakers, it is imperative that those who do have a knowledge of Gaelic are given ample opportunity to express themselves in their own language.

At the planning stage of any theme or project it may be that I do not write-in the Gaelic element. This is because it is understood to be an integral part of the whole and that fluent speakers will have an opportunity to talk, read or write in their own language at all times. I may not even mention it in the plan, which seeks to integrate the whole curriculum, but it is understood that it will form the basic part of all work.

First of all we spoke about the various people who helped us in this area. We discovered that there was so much to learn that we could have done a project on each one. We began with the postman. "Why does he come?" "What does he wear?" "What does he bring?" I was amazed at one boy's response to this last question. He gave, "sheep papers", "money for the wedder", "telephone bills", when I expected only "letters". This sparked off the interest of the other children and we found ourselves making a long list of all the different things that come by the postman's hand. They spoke to the postman and found out about the mail-bus and all the different things. After this, we visited the local postmistress and questioned her about every aspect of her work. She was very patient and co-operative. We bought some stamps and, on our next visited posted some postcards and letters which the children had written. They watched while the letters were date stamped and they examined those and questioned the postmistress about this. During those interviewing sessions the language used was the one which came naturally to each child. The interviewee could switch naturally from one to the other so I expect these interviews could be said to have been truly bilingual. The children then brought in postcards and envelopes from different places and studied the date stamps.

This theme developed on similar lines with other members of the community, e.g. the nurse, local minister, being interviewed and information about their work being sought out by the children at home or from any available sources.

Most of the writing which arose at this time was done in English. Because of the influence of the unusually high proportion of English speakers in the class, I felt it would be more beneficial to the bilingual children to be exposed to the Gaelic language through much more talk and discussion. I had to make a conscious effort all the time to ensure that Gaelic was being developed through discussion, and hence Gaelic writing was pushed outside the theme. This does not mean that it was being neglected, as 'Breakthrough' forms part of the total work programme, and this caters for reading and writing and indeed for further discussion opportunities. I have also devised Gaelic word-games, usually in the form of a quiz and they are very enthusiastic about these. In this way I hope to build up a basic vocabulary for all children on which further work can be based.

Drama was sometimes used as a means of language development and here they themselves were responsible for setting up situations in which e.g. the nurse would have a major part. I noticed the girls were particularly good at this; the boys required more direction.

I very much enjoy this mode of working, where such a great deal of talk and discussion takes place and where children become involved with other members of the community. I feel nearer to the children and feel that I have a deeper insight into the way that children learn, and the problems which they have.

Being involved in the Bilingual Project has meant that the whole curriculum has been opened up for bilingual children. The Gaelic language is seen as an added skill which the children have, and which they can use to extend their understanding of topics and concepts. They are able to extend the discussion because of their skill in language and this is to everyone's benefit. I approve whole-heartedly of the child-centred, experiential approach advocated by the Project for a number of reasons: it gives a chance to less able children who would have difficulty learning from books, it puts the children on a level with each other and gives every child an equal chance, it gives them such a lot to talk about and subsequently to write about and most importantly it gives the children a lot of satisfaction and confidence.

Case Study 10
This is a 1-teacher primary school with 11 pupils. It is situated in a fishing community. Gaelic is the first language of the community and school. There is only 1 pupil in the school whom I class as a Learner. His mother is an English speaker and his father is a Gaelic speaker. I class him as a Learner because he speaks English with his mother at home.

I have been teaching in this school now for 26 years; the school has been the full 6 years in the Bilingual Project. I first began working through the medium of Gaelic in 1963 under the direction of Mr Murdo MacLeod, HMI who was then Gaelic Adviser. As time went by working through themes as 'Centres of Interest' I began to realise their value. I realised that this was a more meaningful and interesting method of working. Work could be done in context on any subject in either Gaelic or English.

When the BEP was set up in 1975 it was exactly what I wanted, what I was looking for, acknowledging and ascertaining that the type of work I had been doing was right. The BEP further developed the work and provided us with welcome help and material. Although I had made use of the environment for teaching purposes previously I had not been digging as deeply into it as I do now in the BEP. We did not go out as often or as far afield. We did not have the added support and resources for environmental work that the BEP now gives us. With the younger children I have always used Gaelic as a medium of instruction because Gaelic was the language that they understood best. In former years as children grew older, however, I gradually introduced English as a medium of instruction so that with the older classes my main medium of instruction was English. Since the setting up of the BEP, however, I continued to use Gaelic as a medium of instruction with older classes so that now Gaelic and English have parity as media of instruction for older classes. With the younger children Gaelic continues to be the medium of instruction.

My present theme of work is 'Time'. I am working on this theme with children throughout the school, both lower and upper primaries, in accordance with the children's level of ability. Work on this theme commenced at the beginning of September and will continue probably into the New Year. It was chosen during the last summer term when I felt that the pupils' concept of 'Time' was rather weak.

I carefully planned and structured my theme before beginning work on it. When the method of planning according to skills and concepts was first introduced to me, what I found difficult was planning from the skills and concepts towards subject matter. It seemed so much easier for me to select the subject matter and then take what I wanted out of that. Having some experience of planning in this way now, however, I realise that the skills and concepts do really come first. I like this particular method of planning very much. I have my work well planned far ahead and this gives me a feeling of security.

Prior to the BEP we were teaching skills and concepts but perhaps we were not as aware of actual skills and concepts as we are now. Perhaps we did not pay as much attention to some of the skills/concepts as we should have . . . and they are invaluable. Once these are established they can be applied in any situation and they remain open to further and further development through Secondary School and into later life.

In this theme 'Time' I have consciously tried to achieve a balance of subjects, also integrating a fiction book namely 'Longtime Passing'. Many skills are being employed through the theme. The children are experiencing and feeling e.g. in their experiences about the use of clocks through the ages — sundials, water clocks, sand clocks. They are interpreting these experiences. They are recording their findings in various ways e.g. by discussion, writing, interviewing, drama. Much researching is also being done. They take photographs, with all the skills involved in that. They do tape-recording, with all the skills involved in that. They do not have any difficulties doing any of these in Gaelic because Gaelic is their first language and the language that comes most naturally to them.

Oral work is done mostly in Gaelic throughout the school although in the case of older children from say P3/4 discussions also take place in English usually preceding English writing.

Reading throughout this theme is done mostly in English because of the lack of Gaelic material available on this particular subject. We do not have the Gaelic resource material that we need and that we want for project work. When doing a theme such as this we make up class books in Gaelic and English of children's findings. These are then used for reading purposes. I do not think that they are yet as advanced in their Gaelic reading as in their English reading. I think this is because they have so many more resources in English than they have in Gaelic. There is also the impact of the media.

From about P3/4, writing on the theme is done in both Gaelic and English. I try to maintain a balance between the two languages for writing purposes. I think that it follows that if the children's Gaelic reading is not as advanced as their English reading, then their Gaelic writing is not as advanced as their English writing. I find a lot of difference now in the infant children's Gaelic writing i.e. P2, 3, 4, this being due to the fact that with them I now use 'Breakthrough' for Gaelic writing. When I first began using it, two or three years before the advent of the BEP I did err with some of the slower children in giving them too many words but after a time I worked out individual requirements and now each child holds what he is capable of handling and no more. With this scheme, the sense of doing and achieving for the child is very, very rewarding. They can read at a very early stage words well within their own vocabulary. They understand what they are reading, it is meaningful to them since it is about things in their own environment. The child does not need to wait until he has mastered the art of writing before he expresses himself in writing. This is very, very important. By the time children reach P3 they can confidently write quite long stories with the help of it. I feel it is too early to take it from them at P2 but at the same time I feel that by the end of P3 some of them are very reluctant to give it up. They seem to be unhappy when the crutch is taken away. This transition stage worries me somewhat and I find that work regresses a little at the beginning of P4. This scheme is of particular benefit to slow pupils and learners: each individual can progress at his own rate.

I feel that with the method of teaching which we now employ i.e. learning at first hand, children give better quality of work both in English and Gaelic. This is because children have something to talk about and so something to write about. This new method provides far more interest, their appetites are whetted, they are more motivated and stimulated, they want to find out more, they feel a freedom to find things out for themselves. Gone are the ranks of children sitting bolt upright not daring to whisper. The classroom atmosphere is much more relaxed. They are allowed to speak to the teacher, to speak to each other, to discuss things together, all providing for better quality of work.

At first when I started doing this type of work, the type of classroom atmosphere described here meant lack of discipline to me. I have no hesitation in saying now, however, that this is definitely not so. A busy class is not an undisciplined class and the best way of keeping discipline is by keeping a class busy and if a class is interested in what they are doing they will be busy. First hand experience provides for exactly this.

My role now is very different to my role in pre-project days when I stood in front of the class and did the telling. Now my role is to manoeuvre classroom discussion in such a way as to get the children to ask questions, to get them interested, to direct them to where they will find an answer to their questions, to get them to do the work. To begin with, adapting to this new role was rather difficult. I needed a lot more patience and often I felt, "I'll just tell them the thing and get on with it." But I realised that if I did that I would not be training them in the skills that they should be trained in . . . skills of researching, skills of recording, skills of experiencing and feeling, skills of interpreting experiences. There are no short cuts.

All my old traditional methods of teaching have also disappeared e.g. reading around the class . . . dry books that quite often children had no interest in, could not understand, did not have feeling for. Spelling is also taught within the context of the theme being studied. Since a great part of our learning resources are found directly in the community there is no doubt that this has affected and altered the relationship between the school and the community. Sadly enough, there are still the few people who think that when we are out of doors we are out 'enjoying ourselves'. Of course we are enjoying ourselves. We are enjoying ourselves very much — but it does not stop there. We come back to the classroom and we do work which we enjoy doing, our outing to the environment having provided us with lively, exciting, interesting work to do.

Many people who have questioned our outings have been amazed to see some of the work we have produced after being out-of-doors. But it is sometimes not so easy to get some of these people who question our work in the environment into school to have a look. They are the more difficult people to get in. Other people take a very active interest in the affairs of the school. They are interested in the outings. When they hear about things which children have seen and found they add to the information. The fact that learning is done in the school environment, however, does not limit, confine or restrict the children's learning to their immediate environment. I have proved over and over again that, on the contrary, from interest and knowledge gained locally, the children's enquiring minds go out all the better equipped to study other communities and lands. The children themselves want to find out more, they want to delve into books. Every skill/concept which one can think of is strengthened by visits to the environment.

On Saturdays children go out by themselves along the beach to see what they can find, and in the summertime, Saturday afternoon has become a time when the school must have an open door because, one after another, children come with something they have found for the school aquarium. It is not just a 5-day week for them, it is a 6-day and possibly a 7-day if they were allowed.

Because there is still such a lack of book resources in Gaelic, we obviously have to prepare more material in Gaelic ourselves. Each separate theme means the making of more materials in the form of reading sheets, class books, word cards etc. We once had a visitor from Norway in the school who questioned that the display on the walls seemed to be in Gaelic. He said, "Bilingual? I do not see much evidence of bilingualism here." I assured him that we were bilingual and that we did a lot of work in English too but that the necessity of preparation of much of our own material in Gaelic meant that Gaelic was more in evidence than English. Also, there is the fact that the children see English everywhere about them and so it is more important that our classroom display be more in Gaelic than in English.

But the situation as regards Gaelic material has definitely changed since the inception of the BEP and this has already made a great deal of difference to the children's reading. These materials have been very well received. They are most effective and we get a lot of work out of them. I find that I am consciously now more discriminating in assessing the worth of materials. I assess them in the light of the skills they afford and the concepts I can reach through them. We need more and more materials, material of every description!

I do not believe, and see no evidence to suggest, that Gaelic has a detrimental effect on their learning of English. After all, when Gaelic is their first language surely if they are taught through Gaelic then they have a much better understanding of what they are doing. I think, therefore, that because they are able to have Gaelic as a medium, their English has, on the contrary benefited. Also, being bilingual their learning experiences are enriched. More than one language makes for enrichment of learning, surely. The children's own attitude to work in Gaelic in school has also changed. To them in olden days Gaelic was treated like a foreign language. It is now accepted by them and they know it is accepted by the school as their first language. They read in it, they speak in it, they write in it, they do everything in it.

When I first embarked on the BEP I did not have any fears. I heard what the work was going to be and the help we were going to get. When I saw the Bilingual Project Team followed that promise up with definite action, rather I welcomed the BEP. I met other teachers. This was invaluable to me. I enjoy meeting other teachers, seeing the work they are doing and exchanging ideas. Getting support from sources outwith one's own classroom is especially useful to a teacher in a 1-teacher school, who has no-one to discuss matters with or share problems. These teachers' meetings have provided a stimulus and although on many occasions I have come home feeling depressed to think of my own efforts in the light of those of other teachers, this has spurred me on to work harder, to develop my work further and to produce more results. I still don't have any fears or qualms about the type of work which I am doing. Although it is very demanding it is also very satisfying and I feel confident that it will continue to be a very successful experiment.

Case Study 11

I am the head teacher in a 2-teacher school of 26 pupils. The school is situated near an army installation. The children come from local and other backgrounds, the majority being local. One half of the school population are fluent Gaelic speakers and the other half offers a range of ability in Gaelic, from P1 entrants with none to fairly fluent learners in P6.

I teach P1-P3 in the school, and in September and October of this year we were studying 'Water'. I chose this topic after yet another day of rain, with the children stuck indoors at playtime. We discussed our need for water and the children recalled their own experiences with various forms of water — ice, snow, steam etc. I decided that since the children showed so much interest, we would use it as a topic. I had no set plan to work to, but I wrote down the work I would like to cover — 1. First hand experiences with water 2. Life in water (We studied the sea.) 3. Experiments with water a) floating and sinking b) capacity c) growing things 4. Stories, rhymes and songs.

I have always approached a topic in this way, using as far as possible the children's interests as a starting point. Within each topic I try to achieve a balance of subjects. In this topic we covered the following subjects in environmental studies — Life in the sea; how water was used in the past to protect castles, duns etc. (ruin on an island in a local loch) Maths — capacity, number e.g. Now many cups of water fill a bucket. Science — floating and sinking, freezing, thawing etc. Language Arts — English and Gaelic stories, rhymes and songs. The majority of the work was carried out in Gaelic as the children are more able to express themselves in their native tongue in the infant room. English was not ignored as I am constantly translating the two languages so that neither Gaelic nor English monoglots miss out on what is being discussed.

I feel that a lot of the children's learning should be based on first hand experience. The children are more enthusiastic if they discover things for themselves. A 1-hour trip to the seaside could teach more about sea creatures than one week's study in a classroom. It makes them more aware and respectful of their own environment, and gives them an opportunity for informal discussion. The children use Gaelic naturally, and it is important that this should be encouraged as native Gaelic speakers come to school with Gaelic names and terms for aspects of their environment, and to ask them to express themselves in another language produces a stilted short sentence lacking in the rich description of their native tongue.

Through discussion the children learn to listen to and learn from one another. From being able to express themselves orally they progress to expressing themselves in writing. Their reading in Gaelic has improved and this can be attributed to the use of 'Breakthrough to Literacy' scheme where they make up sentences from words in their own personal folders. The children have plenty opportunity for reading in Gaelic, but, although the amount of material in Gaelic has improved there is still no graded reading scheme. Although the content of some of the new materials is suitable, the vocabulary proves difficult. The result is that by P3 they are more advanced in English reading than in Gaelic. This is an area of Gaelic learning that requires more attention. Another area requiring more attention is the lack of materials for use with Gaelic learners. In an ordinary class a teacher could have three learners at entirely different stages of learning, but in a composite class the problem is multiplied.

Learning through Gaelic has no detrimental effect on their learning through English. By coming to terms with a problem through their own language, they go on to learn more about it from books written in English and are able to talk and write about it in either language.

Involvement in the project has meant official backing for the kind of teaching I was trained to do, and which I enjoy. Where teachers in the past concentrated on perfecting English grammar through textbooks and exercises, practically ignoring the children's native language, we are now able to teach them a wealth of subjects through their native language, and as a result they acquire a mastery of both the Gaelic and English language.

The classroom atmosphere is relaxed with the children talking natural-ly in both languages. The Gaelic monoglots entering P1 would in the past have felt left out with English so much to the fore. Now everyone in the classroom is equal.

Case Study 12

This primary school is a very old school which has recently been modernised from a single classroom to a 2-floor, 2-classroom plus resource area arrangement.

The catchment area consists of two townships within a distance of 3 miles of the school. It is a scattered crofting community and is a participant in the Council Housing Action Scheme. There are no community centres apart from the church and the school, which is used for Brownies, Girl Guides, concerts, whist drives etc.

Most of the families are economically supported by croft work. Out of the nine families which supply the school, four of the families have work outside the community. Only two of the mothers are employed and that is on a part-time basis. Therefore, with the average size of family being five, there is not much money to spend on material luxuries. One point perhaps worth noting is that the children rarely have the opportunity to leave the community to visit other areas.

After finishing college in 1968, I taught in a primary school on the mainland for three years, then in a Western Isles town school (Storno-way) for four years. I left teaching in 1975 to raise a family and did not return to teaching until August 1980 when I became employed in this school as a supply teacher, teaching primaries 1-4. I now teach primaries 5-7; I have been working with them for one term. Therefore I can only speak with one term's experience of teaching older children in the Bilingual Project. There are 14 pupils of mixed ability in my class. 5 of them have learning difficulties. There are 4 children on P5, 4 children on P6 and 6 children on P7. Of the 14 children, 2 are learners of Gaelic, that is, on entry to school they had none. Their mother has no Gaelic, but their father has.

In my theme of work this term, I especially wanted to compare and contrast the local area here with another minority culture. With the help of BEP fieldworker I decided that 'Julie of the Wolves' by Jean George was the fiction book which would provide me with a starting point to my theme. I had my work planned well in advance: I had planned it in accordance with the skills/concepts approach. I found that this method of planning was a good idea. My first impressions were that it looked rather complicated and involved, but on further study it seemed a logical and organised way to approach the study — the danger, I felt, may have been that organisaion could become the be-all and end-all and that it could become too teacher orientated; scope must be left for spontaneity and initiative.

In the book, we read about an Inuit/Eskimo child bride who finds herself lost in the Tundra on the North Slope of Alaska, running away from her husband who is retarded. It had been an arranged marriage.

We did some work on climate, especially permafrost, cold deserts, Arctic conditions, discussion about thermometers, work on differences in temperature required for e.g. baking, growing, preservation of food by deep freezing. Comparisons made with our own climate conditions. Investigations made to find out methods of food preservations in our own community prior to mechanisation. Work done on direction finding.

Julie learns to communicate with a pack of wolves. Work done on communication — speech; 'Co Iad?' (BBC Schools) tapes on communication used i.e. 'A' Chlann Fhiadhaich' (The Wild Children) and 'Washoe'; telephone; letter; radio/telex; police visited school. At all stages reference and comparisons made to life in the local community.

Animals and birds of the Tundra studied; migration; short summer (24 hour sunlight); winter darkness; study of animals adapting to surroundings; camouflage; how Inuit adapted to harsh Arctic conditions; their food, clothing, shelter, fuel. Transport — dog sledge; snow mobile; aeroplane; — effect on community. Comparisons made with our own local community and the skills necessary for survival in our own community.

Work done on a modern Inuit community — Greenland, houses, transport, employment, food, illness, white man problems, clash of two cultures. Comparisons made with outside influences on our own community. A visit was arranged for a retired Health Visitor to come to the school. She had spent many years in Igloolik in the Eastern Arctic as a nurse. She brought to school with her a display of various examples of Eskimo culture e.g. model of igloo, Eskimo costume, books and many slides to illustrate aspects of the life of the Inuit.

Children's work is recorded in various ways. We made booklets about the Igloolik community, depicting the main aspects of the environment, made wolf poems, made a frieze of Inuit life as it was, made a frieze of life in our own community, food chains etc.

Work is done in both languages on the theme. Most of the informal discussion is carried out in Gaelic. I feel that developing skills of discussion is very important since it develops their spoken language, imagination, logical thought processes, increases their self-confidence, consideration for others and conversational manner.

While pupils have the opportunity to use Gaelic throughout the school day, there are occasions when I encourage them to discuss solely in English to improve their fluency in English e.g. when we are studying an English passage in depth as in 'Scope for Reading'. I myself use Gaelic most of the time in the classroom. It is the official language of the school playground and classroom. The children make the routine informal requests and receive instructions in Gaelic. I have to make a conscious effort to converse in English with my pupils since they themselves have no desire to speak the English language. The only English they hear is that which they hear in school and on television.

Because of the children's greater fluency in Gaelic than in English, it is inevitable that more areas of the curriculum are tackled in Gaelic than in English. So all subjects as far as possible are taught partly in Gaelic. There are difficulties for example in mathematics where specialised vocabulary is predominantly English. At the present moment the work on the walls is pretty balanced between Gaelic and English. Sometimes this is not the case. At times there is more English on the walls and vice versa. But I would say that Gaelic is used right across the curriculum. Gaelic is used to help their English skills.

I try to achieve a balance as far as written work is concerned. I try to get them to write in Gaelic at least 3 times a week. Much preparation has to be done before children write on a theme in Gaelic because of the lack of simple dictionaries and wordlists. There is sometimes difficulty in locating imaginative Gaelic passages suitable for the theme. I can not pass comment on the writing of children in my class prior to the project because I was not here. I did not have previous experience of using Gaelic as a teaching medium, prior to my present position; I had never even taught native Gaelic speakers before. But, through discussions at bilingual meetings, I believe the Gaelic writing of children here is on a par with work produced by other schools.

In Gaelic reading, I would say the children are as advanced as they are in English i.e. their word recognition is equally good, but their comprehension in Gaelic is more advanced. We have a fairly wide selection of Gaelic books in the school, and so they read a full range of written materials ranging from captions on the wall, word lists, our own written materials, and books. Pupils make full use of all available Gaelic materials. Most of our reference books are in English, so guidance as to how to make the best use of them is given in Gaelic. The children also help to provide ideas and inspiration for preparing additional class materials. Of course, one can never have enough Gaelic books — more on environmental studies would be appreciated, as would books of a recreative variety that pupils could read themselves, and some that teachers could read to pupils.

I feel that first hand experience wherever possible is the ideal, but in this last theme we studied, by its very nature, a greater dependence on second hand experience is inevitable. However, when similarities could be drawn with their own area or when speakers visit the school with souvenirs, exhibits etc, it was obvious that first hand experience brought out their most enthusiastic and excited responses.

This is a very close community and the children are very interested in their environment. There is evidence that when they are engaged in a study such as this that they experience great depths of feeling for characters fictional and otherwise in similar situations. The differences and similarities in the environment being studied makes them aware of their own — e.g. Inuit having to seek employment in the cities, not able to have interviews in their own language. Quite a few of the children have shown an interest outwith school hours — by looking for aspects of the theme in publications and bringing their evidence into school; by interviewing parents; by bringing to school items found on the beach of Canadian origin, which previously they would have ignored. Generally, their appreciation of the locality and their powers of observation have been increased.

From my relatively brief experience in this community, I can say that parents seem to approve of this new role of the teacher. I am not sure that they fully appreciate the learning situation but they do not express disapproval. Parents seem to become more involved through pupils' fresh attitudes to their work.

I myself feel it is beneficial for the children to be bilingual. Non-Gaelic-speaking pupils find that learning Gaelic is the passport to becoming accepted in the community. Learners here seem to be fluent when they reach the P4 stage. This is typified by a family of five children who, on entry to school had no Gaelic and a non-Gaelic-speaking mother. I have enjoyed being involved with the project. Visits from project fieldworkers and meetings with other teachers are vitally important, especially for teachers in small schools; a problem shared is a problem halved. The project fieldworkers provide an excellent back-up service, making a wide variety of resources readily available, often at very short notice!

Teachers and pupils are more involved in the learning situations because of the wide range of learning materials used e.g. books, films, demonstrations, tape-recordings, visiting speakers etc. There is more of a community spirit in the classroom. The teacher has to ensure that resources are readily available, and offers guidance and assistance as required, but teacher and pupils are involved in learning together.

I am not in a position to comment on whether the children's attitude to Gaelic has changed, but I can say what it is now. They are very proud of their own language and hold it in very high esteem, perhaps even resent having to learn English. They are very self-confident, very forthcoming, and I have the same friendly relationship with them as I had with monoglots on the mainland and in a town school in the Western Isles. They are certainly not 'reticent island children'. Using the Gaelic language in this kind of learning is very important because it is their mother tongue. I believe that the use of Gaelic has increased their confidence in English as well as Gaelic. Also the children seem to learn more because of the variety of approaches.

Case Study 13
This is a 2-teacher school. I teach P1-P4 classes.

When I launched out on the Bilingual Project with the above classes in 1975, I was not at all sure what it was all about. I had no idea what theme to choose, and I felt completely lost. Anyway after a lot of thought I chose the theme 'The Old Watermill' — remembering my own grandfather as a miller grinding corn and grain into oatmeal and barley-meal. I tried to make it as simple as I could, giving them the Gaelic for various parts of the mill etc, but still I felt I was forcing myself and my words on the children.

After some meetings with other teachers in the working party, things began to take on a different shape. I saw how the others were tackling it, each teacher in her own different way according to the children's background and environment, the children at home, in class, at play after school, at work after school. So in this respect, I found the meetings with other teachers under the supervision of the Bilingual Project staff in North Uist very helpful.

This kind of work was very different from what I used to do in Gaelic. Before, we were confined to the classroom and only reading and a little writing was done. The environment was not taken into account and not much discussion was held with the children. All subjects were kept separate e.g. English on a certain day, History on another, Geography on the next, etc, and also different jotters for each subject. Now we can have discussions in every subject on one day since there is more integration of subjects, and Gaelic is used in all of them. Consequently I find myself very much nearer to the children and they are nearer to me. They are more prepared to come to speak to me and they are more prepared to give their own opinion about anything which is discussed.

By participating in the Bilingual Project we were required to make more use of the environment than before. I now think it is very important that children's learning should be based on first-hand experience. I did not realise this until I took them outside the classroom to examine the environment e.g. to the stream for water-study, into the playground, to the shore etc. Two or three years ago I was doing a theme from a Gaelic programme during which a lot of discussion cropped up about islands. After a good deal of discussion I asked the children to define an island, to tell what really constitutes an island, and no one was able to give me a correct definition. It was when I took them out and showed and discussed with them the different islands round about that they realised what an island is. That instance helped to prove to me the importance of direct experience learning in their own environment and that it also helps them in understanding of other environments.

Over the years we have done a good deal of outside work, visiting, probing, and examining the shore, the hills and the streams. They love to go out, and they notice many things which before would have gone unnoticed. Before, in some instances, they would just have a mental picture; now, they can contact and examine the real thing. Many skills are involved, including, for example, mathematical skills being put into practice. The children have become more and more involved with the shapes, sizes, length, breadth of things; the number of objects found; initiation to sets in maths; weighing different materials like pebbles, sand etc; examining shapes of houses and learning about rectangles, squares, triangles, circles; and a host of other things pertaining to mathematical skills. I see now there is a lot of value in teaching these skills in the local environment; the children are more ready to notice and compare things, and to ask about anything they do not understand. It has also benefitted their learning outwith school. I would also mention that there is a carry-over of this kind of work done in Gaelic to work done in English.

I believe that the crux of the development of skills is the opportunity for discussion. Before, the teacher gave, and the children received. Now, it is the other way round, the children give and the teacher helps. When anything difficult crops up and a solution is needed, it is good to hear the children giving their opinion and even arguing about it. For example, a

147

child says one of the animals found in Greenland is a camel; another child immediately contradicts this statement saying "A camel could not live in Greenland," and then the argument is started, and the whole subject is thrashed out with the help of the teacher. The discussion then leads to hot and cold countries, desert, Arctic Circle etc; different countries are discussed and compared and a whole Geography lesson is taught, stemming from one child's mistake. This is how I find the role of the teacher different nowadays. The kind of talk the teacher does is quite different.

I have a lot of 'learner' Gaelic children in my classroom; in fact, they outnumber the native speakers. To begin with I have to use a lot of simple Gaelic with these children, e.g. getting them to understand and carry out simple commands like "give me the kettle" or "shut the door". They have many other opportunities for developing the skill of talking in Gaelic, such as relating simple stories of their own experience to the class e.g. about the situation in their homes in the morning, what they had for breakfast, something funny that happened at home. They have little dialogues with one another on the toy telephone. We act out little plays involving much repetition of words and phrases. These situations are entirely different to what we used to do.

The children's writing in Gaelic has greatly improved, especially in the amount that they can write about any subject. Some of them experienced problems at first with spelling and grammar. The spelling problems were overcome with more attention being given to Gaelic phonics. The learners who experienced difficulty with grammar and sentence formation gradually improved through plenty repetition and practice. The quality of their writing, both factual and creative, has also improved immensely and I attribute this to — their learning being based on direct experience and use of the environment; having had stories read to them; listening to radio programmes both Gaelic and English; having had a lot of discussion on various themes. They also had increased opportunity for writing in Gaelic.

Children's reading in Gaelic has also improved a great deal. I can only attribute this to the increased number of Gaelic books they now have access to. I seem to notice recently that they are more advanced in Gaelic reading than they are in English reading. In fact, they prefer reading in Gaelic because the Gaelic books seem to pertain to the children's own background, whereas the English reading books are more alien to them and the stories are not anything near to their own background. When the project began, the staff of the project made up simple texts based on the work of the children. These were tried out in the schools, revised and illustrated, and then published as simple reading books which the children really love to read. The supply of Gaelic material from the project has made a great difference to their reading ability. This material is always received with pleasure and is very effective. I find myself also becoming more involved in preparing Gaelic classroom material, and more discriminating in assessing the content of Gaelic material.

The children's experiences are recorded in many different ways — through discussion, writing, frieze-making and other art-work, drama, photography, tape-recording, tape/slides using slide films and ektagraphic slides.

I do not think the relationship between the school and the community has altered in any way. The parents take an interest in the affairs of the school and understand the kind of teaching being done, but they are inclined to leave it to the confines of the classroom. Hardly any Gaelic is spoken in the homes. Once the children go out of the classroom at the end of the school day, most of them do not hear another word of the language until the next day.

I do not think that learning through Gaelic has any detrimental effect on the children's learning in English; in fact I think their English learning has gained. I feel it is beneficial for the children to be bilingual, and also that non-Gaelic speakers should learn the language.

Case Study 14

Our primary school is housed alongside the secondary department and although ours is a Gaelic speaking area it is mostly English spoken in the playground due to a majority of incomers.

There are two primary teachers and a roll of 44 pupils. I teach Primaries 4-7, a total of 23 pupils. Of these, 9 pupils receive remedial teaching and there is also a mentally handicapped child in the class. Only 8 pupils come from a completely Gaelic-speaking home, nine have one parent who can speak Gaelic and the rest have no Gaelic background.

I have only been teaching this group for five weeks and I am still getting to know some of them and renewing my acquaintance with the others. I am finding it extremely difficult to come to terms with having such a large class in which there are so many slow learners and pupils with personality problems. I have not yet begun work on a particular theme so I shall comment on how the project has affected my teaching before now.

One of the interesting features I have discovered through the project is to look into our own locality for themes and topics. These are so close to us they could easily be overlooked — life in a nearby loch or dyke, history of our school, local industry, world war history, crofting etc. Information and experience is so accessible that the children readily collect it from their families and surroundings and it is far easier to guide them properly when dealing with familiar subjects. In my classroom we once

149

had a good collection of wartime photographs and other items. We also had a collection of stones, containers etc from the beach.

Within the past year I have come to realise that planning of a theme is very important. A few minutes spent outlining different aspects, subjects, skills, aims to be taught are invaluable. I frequently refer to my plan and sometimes I see that changes have to be made according to our progress. It is important to remember that each skill must be thoroughly taught before moving on to the next.

My method of teaching Gaelic has become a whole new world since the beginning of the project. In the past I would revert to methods used in my own schooldays, mainly isolated reading lessons. I cannot stress enough how the standard of written Gaelic in my classroom has improved and last year the creative writing of P7 was on a par with their English work. With the work done in the infant room as a basis the children build up individual vocabularies at their own levels and continuity is natural. They have my help and that of each other in writing difficult words.

When working on a theme I use several methods of recording/communicating which I find useful. The most common ones are discussion, observation, writing, blackboard and picture making. I know I am not making adequate use of the tape recorder and the camera. Drama is a favourite and I now have 2 or 3 pupils who have developed an interest in it.

From time to time my fellow teacher and I discuss our work plans, reviewing aims and the skills being taught. Since we have begun this method I find that I get far better continuity in my work, especially in language arts, discussion skills and social skills.

The situation in our township has changed such that our primary school now consists mostly of learners of Gaelic, whereas at the inception of the project almost everyone was Gaelic speaking. I am now finding that I shall have to change my teaching tactics to accommodate this and I am at present considering how best to approach things. I can see that plenty repetition and patience will be required.

I would not like to have to change from the thematic approach we have developed because the standard of written Gaelic has so improved, creative writing in English has been enriched and the children's awareness of themselves and their immediate environment has been awakened.

Case Study 15
I was not in the least confident in the beginning and I felt so inadequate that I preferred to blunder along on my own rather than have contact with teachers from other schools. I sometimes felt quite confused after the meetings but what I did find useful was the Bilingual Project advisers visiting the school and seeing what one was actually attempting to do,

pointing out the faults and good points and giving concrete advice. I feel that the security of one's own classroom is more favourable for this type of help. Discussion with teachers in one's own school is very important as apart from knowing what 'subjects' the other classes are covering it is also good to talk about problems, successes, etc. It is also good to hear from Bilingual Project advisers about any good approach teachers in other schools have, as one can benefit from studying this or even copying it.

A few years ago there was gasps of dismay from the children and signs of despair from me when it was time for Gaelic on the timetable. Although the children could read quite well it was all so terribly uninteresting, but what really pained me was the terrible Gaelic writing. The children were at the 'ha' for the 'tha' stage and apart from the odd child's work the written work was really poor and my head ached at the thought of correcting.

Now, however, their Gaelic work has improved and with it the teacher/pupil relationship. The children wrote so much and spoke so little before, but now the emphasis has changed and as a result the whole atmosphere of the classroom is more friendly, and the children have become more forthcoming and confident. Our work is so much more interesting as the children have become more motivated.

The children love learning by first-hand experience through using the locality or environment. Here even the children who are not very intelligent can feel quite important as they might be the ones who can catch that slippery eel or who can handle beetles that the teacher and other pupils are afraid to touch. Our study of mini-beasts, a stream, part of the seashore and the fishing industry was extremely pleasant work.

When we began the fishing project we were given a plan which it was suggested we could follow. From this plan, we first selected 'the adaptation of man to his environment'. I found this method of planning very helpful indeed because not only were we given a variety of concepts which we could study but also many examples of how each concept could be linked to content. It is this kind of planning which helps one to make a success of a project. It also encourages the use and development of many skills.

I began this project by discussing in Gaelic with the children how fishing became the livelihood of the men who came to live here because of the excellent fishing grounds surrounding the island. Under discussion was how the fishing survived and is still the main livelihood on the island although other industries such as weaving, knitting with machines and crofting — except on a small scale — did not succeed. Where possible, discussions were in Gaelic and more than half the children were able to express their views in Gaelic whilst some of the other children spoke both Gaelic and English and two or three spoke in English. We began a class booklet and one of the girls recorded in it the context of the discussion we had had. From there we went on to discuss our six local fishing boats. We pasted photographs of these and wrote some details in our booklet, such as the number of men working on each boat and what each man does, where the boat was built, how much it cost, etc. Shortly after this we discussed how families adapted to the men being away from home. One boy from Primary 6 took a tape-recorder home and his mother did a Gaelic recording relating to how the women became quite expert at doing the chores that the man of the house would normally do, such as fixing a washing line or seeing to a broken window, etc.

Meantime the children were busy studying the different types of fish they were seeing on the fishing boats and catching whilst rock fishing themselves. The children's interest in that led them to make a wall-frieze. Most of the children made individual pictures of fish and a small group made a background which was a cross-section of the fishing grounds. The various kinds of fish were then pasted on to the appropriate background on the frieze. Flat fish at the bottom, fish caught whilst rock fishing near the surface, and the remaining kinds in between. Knowledge of where the various kinds of fish were found in the sea was acquired partly from first hand experience and partly from English reference books. They knew most of the Gaelic names of fish from hearing them at home and they knew the most common English ones as well.

A study of the trawl net, drift net, seine net, purse net and the line net took place, and whilst the girls were at needlework one afternoon, the boys made a painting of the different nets and wrote about these. The children were familiar with the trawl net and the long line which are used by the local fishermen and they had to look up English reference books for the others. The children are very adept at this method of getting information. I believe that their reference skills were greatly helped by the study of mapping which took place during the second year of the Bilingual Project. They learned to make use of an index and use grid reference numbers. The older children help to pass these skills on to the younger ones and I think this is an important advantage of composite classes.

From there we went on to talk about the daily timetable of a fisherman and what time actually meant to fishermen. Here we were helped with details by one of the fathers who gave a good account in Gaelic of the daily timetable on a tape. We played the tape and recorded the information in our booklet. A great deal of the children's time is spent aboard the fishing boats when they are in harbour so I was listening to much discussion about the gear on the boats. It is obvious that the boys especially, knew what they were talking about so I gave them a camera to take some

152

photographs of the equipment. Primary 5 and Primary 7 boys made two models of the fishing boats with some equipment.

During this time the children were bringing in copies of the 'Fishing News'. I think their interest in the 'Fishing News' was greatly influenced by their home attitude to the paper and the importance they place on it. It seems to be a very popular paper on the island although I would not buy it myself. Some of them would point out articles about the 'foreigners', etc. on bringing the paper to school, so obviously they are listening to discussion at home. This was especially evident at the time of the strike. They were personally involved because the fathers were not bringing money home and they were very interested in what was going on.

From these papers we cut out any interesting articles and pasted them on to sheets of paper. In this way there was reading material available for everyone and the children found it easier to read separate articles than the complete newspaper. From the newspaper headlines, the television and the radio the children learned that the 'foreigners' were ignoring the measures which were taken to prevent overfishing such as the quota, limits and bans on fishing certain fish and were thus partly responsible for the poor state of the fishing market. As a result the French, Dutch, etc. became very unpopular. A boy on Primary 7 did a Gaelic interview with one of the men on his father's boat and he told how the 'foreigners' abused all measures which were taken to help the fishing industry but that it was the Common Market rules that was the real cause of the deterioration of the fishing industry. All this was recorded in our booklet. Meanwhile the fishermen had taken industrial action because of the poor prices they received for the fish and one of the fishermen told us on the tape how they just wanted a decent price for the fish landed. They did not want much, but they did not gain anything by their industrial action. They had to go back to work as a little money was better than nothing. The children realised from the 'News' that our fishermen were well off compared to fishermen on the mainland; some of these were not able to pay for the cost of running the boats and had to give up fishing and their boats just lay idle. On television they saw good programmes showing lovely big boats lying idle because the owners could not afford to run them. However, the fact that a new fishing boat was bought at that time in such a small island helped them to realise that our fishermen weren't badly off.

We went on to discuss the location of the two harbours. Why was the North Harbour used for the fishing boats only when they are being cleaned and painted? Why do they use the Acarsaid Harbour all the time? We posed these questions and then went to look at both harbours. The children then through observation realised that the Acarsaid Harbour was navigable at all states of the tide but the North Harbour is very shallow and the foreshore dry at low tide. Whilst we were at the harbour we collected pieces of net and rope, etc. The children arranged some of these into the shape of some sea creatures e.g. jelly-fish, star-fish, sea-urchin, etc. and made a collage.

Later we spoke about food-chains. We intended one big food-chain but this was quite difficult as we were not too sure about what each fish ate so we made different food-chains for the animals which we were certain about. One went like this: Man → whale → shark → tuna → herring→ mackerel→ animal→ plankton→ plant plankton. Awareness rather than facts learned (Concept of food-chain). We discussed how numerous the enemies of the fish were and we made a wall-frieze of some of these. We also spoke about the effect of pollution such as oil-spills, sewage and seepages from chemical factories, etc. and how mass deaths of fish were caused by these. We spoke about how the very efficient fishing equipment and gear had made life so much easier for the fishermen than it had been in the olden days when they had very little or no equipment.

Our discussion on food-chains and pollution was in Gaelic but we spoke about pollution and the fishing equipment mostly in English as so many technical terms were involved. We discussed partly in Gaelic, partly in English how the design of the boats and the material used in boat construction have changed very little although much steel is used now and also ferro-cement. We got the information on the construction of boats in the 'Fishing News' and also from a Gaelic interview which one of the Primary 5 girls made with her father.

When the children talk amongst themselves they seem to talk a great deal of English but they change to Gaelic, those who are able, as soon as the teacher joins in.

Now we went on to study how the fishing follows a seasonal pattern and how different gear is used for different fish. The father of one of the Primary 7 boys gave us very good information on a Gaelic tape recording. He told us how the sprats gather together and come in near the shore at the beginning of Spring; he also told how one cannot catch prawns unless it is light as they sleep in the soft clay at the bottom of the sea in the dark. This fisherman also took good photographs for us of the fish being hauled into the boat, emptied on the deck and sorted. We hope to get photographs of the whole procedure from the casting of the net to the fish being sold at the market before the end of the summer. We also learned about the usefulness of the compass and the plimsoll line.

Whilst they were writing a poem one child pointed to a fish on the frieze and said you'd think that fish was chasing the one in front. In no-time the children had made up a couple of verses about the fish on the wall-frieze. The children write very good poems and creative stories about the fish and fishing. Before the children wrote their poems and stories I read a relevant piece of prose and verse to them to motivate them and then we had a discussion in Gaelic about the readings and the subject which they were going to write about. I feel that the discussion before their writing is very important as it seems to help the quality of their work. Learning through first-hand experience is very good for the children.

I believe that this theme was enjoyed by all because nothing was too much effort for the children. They were prepared to give up their time in the evenings and at week-ends to find out any information required. I feel that it was enjoyed so much because it was a subject that the whole family could get involved in. The fact that their parents were involved must have surely helped the children. It also made me realise that the parents were only too willing to help seeing they had good knowledge of the subject. Whereas before I thought the parents were unhelpful, I now know that like myself they probably just suffered from lack of confidence because of lack of knowledge of the subject we were studying. Even after the theme was completed the children still showed interest by bringing any article or information pertaining to the theme to the school or to my home after school hours.

The children's skill in Gaelic writing has greatly improved. Spelling was a great problem but we managed to overcome that by constantly displaying the words which would be commonly used in a certain project on the blackboard, on the wall and in personal dictionaries where they kept alphabetically listed words. The quality of the writing has improved owing I think to the lengthy discussions which take place before they write. Without the discussions, fewer would produce good pieces of writing. The children's Gaelic reading was quite good even before the Bilingual Project began, but as we read more interesting books oftener, and as the children themselves read stories and writings related to the project displayed on the wall, their reading has become more interesting and much better.

Learning through Gaelic has not had any detrimental effect on the children's learning in English. Those who produce good work in Gaelic also produce good work in English.

I feel it is beneficial for anyone who is living in a bilingual area to have the two languages especially if they are going to live in such an area for any length of time.

6. Project Outcomes

In the case studies the teachers gave an account of how they themselves and the work in their classrooms fared within the context of the project. In enabling teachers to try out new methods the project had to build up an atmosphere where teachers could discuss their work openly with colleagues and with the team, and where they attempted new modes of working with the children. The case studies speak for themselves in showing the very many ways in which teachers took new and exciting steps in implementing the alternative curriculum. The project generated a feeling that things were happening and that everyone involved was attempting to break new ground. Teachers were seeking answers for themselves, and looked to colleagues and to the team for confirmation. Teachers were being asked to consider, and even to change, the very criteria by which they had valued what went on in school.

The project team utilised issues such as 'planning' to encourage the teachers to consider what they were trying to do as well as to anticipate how best to do it. Themes such as 'oral skills' and 'experiential learning' provided lengthy discussion at team meetings. The case studies reflect the ways in which teachers incorporated many such themes into their everyday work with the children. The role of the teacher as one who guides and helps rather than one who merely "tells it all" arises frequently in the teachers' accounts. Where teachers have been able to implement these and related ideas they have commented often on the children's increased level of motivation and achievement, as well as on the friendly relationship between the children and the teacher. In such cases a happy, active learning environment has been created.

What the teachers were being asked to do was neither simple nor easy. They were being encouraged to introduce changes in the content of the curriculum, to incorporate knowledge which was to be gleaned from

156

community resources as much as, if not more than, from books. They were being asked to contribute relevant teaching materials linked to that content. They were being asked to anchor the work of the school in the everyday life of the children in the villages. They were being asked to adopt a teaching style which stressed the child's potential for sustained personal learning. And they were being asked to aid the child in developing all aspects of two linguistic codes against an evolving pattern of skills and concepts. Measured against such a matrix, the achievements documented in the case studies are all the more encouraging.

The changes that have taken place in the curriculum of primary schools in this country since the early 1960's towards a more child-centred discovery-learning approach have emanated mainly from individual classrooms. This has resulted in a general pattern of development which shows a wide range of style and pace. The case studies show that the pattern of curriculum reform achieved within this project reflects the wider national pattern. This is not surprising since the project adopted a mode of working which relied on teacher participation and development rather than attempting to impose change from the centre. Where project classrooms differ from the overall picture is in the extent of change within a relatively short period of time. The mechanism of the project provided a means of support for teachers, which speeded up the process of change in the schools.

The accounts given of the extent of the children's learning within the new curriculum show it to be as significant as the gains for the teacher. The teachers have found that the children have gained in motivation and in their knowedge, based on their environment, and that they have become skilled in discovery learning and its related reference skills. Not surprisingly, their skills in Gaelic in all dimensions, from oral work to reading and writing, have improved, alongside their developing skills in using English. The case studies document the many ways in which the skills in both languages are being utilised and extended within the new curriculum. In developing the child's skills in Gaelic the teachers note numerous obstacles which hinder normal regular progress, not least the lack of support from outwith the school.

The communities in which the project schools are set vary considerably in the degree to which Gaelic or English is used as the language of ready discourse in the home and in the village. In certain communities parents have returned from the mainland and tend to use English. In other communities a number of non-Gaelic speakers have taken up residence. The range of situations is highlighted where one case study states that the children's use of English is confined to the school and in another community the children's use of Gaelic is confined to the school. Consideration of the profile of children's facility in the two languages within any given school has to take into account the pattern of language use in that community. The background is made more complex in that almost all parents who choose to speak English in the home wish their children to become skilled in Gaelic, through the school. Also, almost all non-Gaelic-speaking parents living in these communities are very eager for their children to learn Gaelic in school. No parent — Gaelic speaker or non-Gaelic-speaker — has expressed the wish to have his or her child excluded from Gaelic work in school.

The Hebridean school like its counterpart on the mainland of Scotland, has yet to make significant progress in informing and involving parents in the life of the school. This had relevance for the new bilingual curriculum as for any other. Had there been a pattern of parent/teacher meetings this would have provided an overall forum for information and discussion. The project would have utilised any existing system linking schools and home: it was not possible for it to create this system. The case studies show how many people in the community, including parents, became involved in ongoing school themes, but this involvement, significant as it was, tended to be patchy.

In implementing the Gaelic dimension of the curriculum most teachers continued to be frustrated by the lack of extensive, varied reference material. In utilising the local environment as a learning resource, teachers were aware of the impossibility of having any localised published materials which would fit this approach and meet their everyday needs, but they felt keenly the lack of Gaelic material of any kind which they could use to develop this approach. Although the project team devoted a good deal of time to the development of materials such as 'Gaelic Breakthrough' and the 'Grian' reading scheme the main concern of the project was with teacher development through discussion on curriculum reform linked to children's needs. Whereas the latter concern was being developed as a social-interaction model where teachers were being encouraged by colleagues, the development of materials required a Research, Development and Diffusion model which was not central to this project's method.

In almost any classroom there were a number of children whose first language was English. The case studies indicate how such children were involved in the new curriculum and how they were being supported so as to gain a basic grounding in Gaelic fluency and literacy. The work of the project has highlighted the need for a comprehensive programme for teaching Gaelic as a second language to young children. Knowing the psycho-biological conclusions regarding the early years as being the 'critical period' for language learning and given that these children live in the Gaelic culture and that their parents wish them to partake of it fully, the need for such a programme is considerable.

Coping with the wide range of Gaelic linguistic ability within each classroom was one of the major problems confronting project teachers. Whereas the most diligent and ingenious coped with it, often in admirable ways, it undoubtedly helped to frustrate the attempts of the less vigorous. There was the added tendency, rather common among teachers, of accepting a child's current level of fluency in Gaelic as being his full potential in the language. "Their Gaelic is so poor" was sometimes taken as the reason for giving up, rather than the base-line from which to begin. Contrast was made in discussion with the situation where a teacher might say of new entrants "Hardly any of them know any mathematics."

The image of the secondary school presented itself as a spectre frequently at teachers' meeting. Again the project was sometimes being asked to cope with a problem — that of reconciling primary and secondary methods — which has been far too enduring for the project to tackle adequately. Undoubtedly it presented problems for teachers in accepting the new curriculum being proposed, to know that a child-centred activity-learning approach was truncated after P7. "Do they give marks in the secondary for oral proficiency?" asked one primary teacher at a meeting.

Particularly at a time of financial stringency teachers were becoming more aware of the need to gear education to maximise the pupil's chances of employment subsequently. Pupils in the Western Isles had for long been educated to cope with a working life away from home. Doubts about the new bilingual curriculum were sometimes expressed as to its relevance for later employment, possibly in an urban setting, and teachers were being encouraged by the popular press to feel that 'a return to the 3 R's' was being proposed by powers that be, to the exclusion of modern child-centred methods.

It is clear that it needed a stout heart to achieve the level of progress depicted in the case studies. Given the awareness of the apparent wider decline of Gaelic, its minimal use in broadcasting, its peripheral role in newspapers, and the perplexing antagonism to it as reflected in the Gaelic Bill in Parliament, teachers had good reason to feel debilitated. Added to these more general issues they were sometimes confronted at teachers' meetings with a range of obstacles which some brought up with predictable regularity: 'they have such poor Gaelic', 'the Gaelic spelling is impossible', 'parents don't speak it', 'secondary teachers just want them to sit quietly and to have learned their tables', 'there are no books'.

Given the swirling attitudes towards all these issues at teachers' meetings it was necessary for project field workers to attend virtually all the meetings throughout the second phase. Added to the changing attitudes towards Gaelic was the range of changing attitudes towards the curriculum as a whole, and the fact that teachers were being involved in an often complex and sometimes difficult exercise. The work that has been done reflects considerable personal commitment by the individual teachers involved.

An interesting feature of this project is that it is being undertaken in a culture which has given special emphasis to traditional values and egalitarianism. This has influence on the emergence of leadership and innovation. Individuals have tended not to put themselves forward either in speech or in action for fear of being seen as 'pushing themseves'. Age, years of experience and gender remain relevant factors. In this rural area people know of each other throughout wide areas of the Islands. This cannot fail to affect the manner in which responsibility is exercised by promoted staff within schools as well as the self-image which people have of themselves in situations such as teachers' meetings.

At the end of the second phase a network of peripheral-peripheral 'cluster' meetings have been established but these are still being organised and led usually by the project team. Lateral contact between schools has been minimal except through these meetings. The achievements in individual classrooms continue to emanate through these meetings and out from there into surrounding schools. Innovation and progress travels from the grass-roots upwards.

7. Beyond The Project

The research and development which the project was established to carry out, like the materials produced by the team, have influenced provision in other Gaelic-speaking areas, but the project's location in the Western Isles has been of central importance to the work. Whatever its application elsewhere, the work of the project has been to develop for primary schools in the Western Isles a more relevant curriculum in line with the best current practice and to explore ways in which such development could be sustained.

The project has carried out its work within the context of the Council's Bilingual Policy and especially paragraphs 3.1 and 3.3 of that policy:

"3.1 **General Aim**
The Council's provision of adequate bilingual education is the most important element in the Council's bilingual policy. It will be the element which makes the greatest demands on the Council's resources, both of finance and of manpower, and which, it is to be expected, makes the greatest impact. The aims of formal education should be to enable children from a Gaelic speaking background to become literate and competent in the use of both Gaelic and English to a level comparable with that achieved in English by their peers elsewhere in the country, and to provide adequate facilities throughout the school for children from a non-Gaelic-speaking background to learn Gaelic as a second language. It has to be recognised that, in pursuit of these aims, a child's educational progress would not, and should not be prejudiced.

3.3 **Primary Education**
The specific aim of the Council in the provision of primary education is that, Gaelic speaking children be as literate and fluent in Gaelic as in English when transferring from primary to secondary education. In their

first years at primary school, Gaelic speaking children will be taught to speak, read and write both Gaelic and English so that they will be able to use both languages as a means of learning. Thereafter, adequate time and resources will be devoted to both languages at all stages of primary school for children to learn Gaelic as a second language in accordance with the wishes of their parents."

It has always been recognised that the scale and range of development required was such that it could not be completed in six years — that the implementation of the Council's bilingual policy in this area of education was a medium to long term undertaking. The project, by focussing attention on this particular area, has made considerable gains and has built up in close co-operation with teachers a significant impetus towards change. There are further steps to be taken in order that the gains made are not lost and further development is assured.

There is a continuing need for consolidation and teacher support. The development of bilingual education is dependent upon the teachers and they are now shouldering more of the burden of development with support and guidance from the project team by visits and meetings. It would be unrealistic at this stage to leave it all to teachers, however.

There is a need to make the resources of the project available to all Western Isles schools. The Project is now operating in 34 schools, although it obviously influences more than that. In some areas 'clusters' of schools operate as units with support from project staff and the creation of more area clusters would benefit the development generating a greater degree of self-reliance.

There is a need for a sustained programme to develop teaching of Gaelic as a second language to children in the primary school. Although the project was not established to cater primarily for the needs of the Gaelic learner, no school in the islands is wholly Gaelic and teachers have been helped to deal with mixed-language classes as the need arose. However, the project has not given this task priority, recognising that it would seriously affect progress with its principal task. In some schools, the basic approach promoted by the project is appropriate but the incidence of fluent Gaelic speakers is so limited that a whole range of suitable materials and techniques requires to be built up.

There is a pressing need for development of materials to support and extend the provision of bilingual education. The project by marshalling skills of teachers and others has broken new ground in ways of preparing and using materials but it is generally acknowledged that the lack of an adequate supply of books and audio-visual materials in Gaelic hinders development.

There is a need to co-ordinate bilingual provision in primary with provision in secondary schools. The present situation as far as the project is concerned is one of organic but not structural links with secondary school: individual teachers in secondary schools have learned from the project and have contributed to its development and most secondary schools use some material prepared by the project. It would be of benefit for the project team to co-operate with an appropriate development team for secondary school.

In December 1981, Comhairle nan Eilean agreed that the project team should continue as a bilingual curriculum development unit within the Education Department to carry out a further 3 year programme of work. The main aims of this phase are — to consolidate further and maintain support for teachers; to extend the work to all Western Isles primary schools; to continue the development of materials; to devise procedures and materials for Gaelic second language learning in the primary school; and, as far as is appropriate, to co-operate with a bilingual education development team for the secondary school if such be established.

References

1 Scottish Education Department, *Educational Research 1976: A Register of Current Educational Research Projects* . . . Her Majesty's Stationery Office 1976.

2 Martin Woodhead, *Co-operation between parents, pre-school and the community*. Council of Europe 1977.

3 Scottish Education Department, *Primary Education in Scotland*. Her Majesty's Stationery Office 1965.

4 Asle Høgmo and Karl Jan Solstad, *The Lofoten Project: Towards a Relevant Education*. University of Tromso 1977.

5 A Bruce Gaarder, *Organisation of the Bilingual School; IN Journal of Social Issue*. 23, 1967. Society for the Psychological Study of Social Issues.

6 Sir Allan Bullock *A Language for Life: Report of the Committee of Inquiry appointed by the Secretary of State for Education and Science*. Her Majesty's Stationery Office 1975.

7 David Mackay, Brian Thompson, Pamela Schaub, *Breakthrough to Literacy Teacher's Manual*. Longman for the Schools Council 1970.

8 Lawrence Stenhouse, *An introduction to Curriculum Research and Development*. Heinemann Educational Books 1975.

9 Derick S Thomson ed. *Gaidhlig ann an Albainn* (Gaelic in Scotland). Gairm Publications 1976.

10 Kenneth Mackinnon, *Language, Education and Social Processes in a Gaelic Community*. Routledge and Kegan Paul 1977.

11 C.V. James ed., *The Older Mother Tongues of the United Kingdom.* Centre for Information on Language Teaching and Research 1978.

12 Comhairle nan Eilean, *Poileasaidh Da-Chananach (Bilingual Policy).* Western Isles Islands Council 1982.

13 Eurwen Price and C J Dodson, *Bilingual Education in Wales 5-11.* Evans/Methuen Educational for the Schools Council 1978.

14 John Murray and Finlay Macleod, "Sea Change in the Western Isles of Scotland: The Rise of Locally Relevant Bilingual Education" in *Rural Education in Urbanised Nations: Issues and Innovations,* edited by Jonathon P Sher. Westview Press 1981.

Appendices

Appendix 1
PROJECT TEAM AND CONSULTATIVE COMMITTEE
MEMBERS 1975-1981

PROJECT TEAM

John Murray	(1975-78)
Catherine Morrison	(1975-81)
Annie MacDonald	(1975-81)
Christina Mackenzie	(1978-81)
Effie MacQuarrie	(1978-81)

CONSULTATIVE COMMITTEE

John A Smith, Vice-Principal, Jordanhill College of Education (Chairman).

John A Macdonald, Gaelic Department, Jordanhill College of Education (until 1979).

Ronald MacDonald, Director of Education, Highland Region (until 1981).

Angus MacLeod, Director of Education, Comhairle nan Eilean (until 1979).

Finlay MacLeod, Depute Director of Education, Comhairle nan Eilean.

Murdo MacLeod, HM Inspector of Schools, Scottish Education Department.

William Nicol, HM Inspector of Schools, Scottish Education Department.

John Nisbet, Professor of Education, University of Aberdeen.

Ronald Richardson, Assistant Principal, Jordanhill College of Education (until 1979).

Thomas R Bone, Principal, Jordanhill College of Education (since 1979).

Neil R Galbraith, Director of Education, Comhairle nan Eilean (since 1979).

Kathleen Macaskill, Chairman, Education Committee (since 1978).

166

David Mackay, Project Consultant (since 1977).
Donald John Macleod, Director, Community Education Project
(since 1979).
John Maclean, Director, Community Education Project (until 1979).
John Murray, Project Co-ordinator, Assistant Director of Education
(Community Education), Comhairle Nan Eilean. (Since 1978).
Donald Martin, Depute Director of Administration, Comhairle nan
Eilean (since 1978).
George Riddell, Vice-Principal, Jordanhill College of Education
(since 1980).
Michael Russell, Project Leader, Cinema Sgire (1978-1980).

Appendix 2

PUBLISHED AND UNPUBLISHED MATERIALS PREPARED AND/OR EDITED BY THE BILINGUAL EDUCATION PROJECT 1975-1981

A. BOOKS.

Tugainn Cuairt Finlay Macleod, illustrations by Jewel B Smith. Published by An Comunn Gaidhealach, 1976.

Leagsaidh Luchag Kenna Campbell, illustrations by Priscilla Campbell. Published by Clo-Beag, 1977.

Cliath series, published by An Comunn Gaidhealach and the Highlands and Islands Development Board, 1977.

   An Nead Kenna Campbell, illustrations by Priscilla Campbell.

   Luasgan Kenna Campbell, illustrations by Jean Haugh.

   Rud a Chunnaic Uiseag Bilingual Education Project, illustrations by Andrew McMorrine.

   Uilleam Bàn agus an Iolair Norman Campbell, illustrations by Donald Smith.

   MacCurraich agus an t-Isean Bilingual Education Project, illustrations by Andrew McMorrine.

   MacCurraich agus am Melodeon John Murray, illustrations by Andrew McMorrine.

Blàir Mhór an t-Saoghail series, published by Oliver & Boyd, 1977.
   Hannibal agus Blàr Loch Trasimene
   Cortes am Measg nan Aztecs
   An Armada
   Blàr Abhainn na Fala
Original texts by Anna Jungmann, illustrations by Doffy Weir, Gaelic adaptation by Finlay MacLeod.

Spàgan series, published by Longman Group Limited in association with the Bilingual Education Project for the Western Isles Islands Council 1978.

Spàgan agus am bike ùr
Spàgan a muigh air a' bhike
Spàgan agus an dealbh
Spàgan aig an t-surcus

Spàgan anns an ospadal
Spàgan air an tràigh
Spàgan ag obair
Spàgan agus a' bhrioscaid

Spàgan air chuairt a muigh
Spàgan aig féill nan toys
Spàgan a' ceannach peata
Spàgan agus an tigh ùr

Original texts by Ellen Blance and Ann Cook, illustrations by Quentin
Blake, Gaelic adaptations by John Murray, Catherine Morrison, Annie
MacDonald and Finlay MacLeod.

O Tractar! Finlay MacLeod, illustrations by Andrew McMorrine (pub-
lished by Acair 1979.)
Coinneach Lisa Storey, illustrations by Roy Pedersen (published by
Acair 1979.)
An Duine Thàinig an Chunntadh nan Tighean Finlay MacLeod, illustra-
tions by Andrew McMorrine (published by Acair 1979.)

Air a' chanal
Air an rathad
Original text by Allan Campbell Maclean. Illustrations by Duncan
Maclaren. Gaelic translation by the Bilingual Education Project. Pub-
lished by Acair 1980.

Grian Early Reading Series
Text by the Bilingual Education Project. Illustrations by Katharine
Barr, Jewel Smith, John Pearson, Christine Macphail. Prepared by
1981. Published by Acair 1982/83.
bàtaichean
iasg
cù beag, cù mòr
Na h-uain
Mo Sheanair
Na Cearcan Ura
Sneachd

An Teaghlach Againn
Làraidh agus Digear
A' Togail a' Bhuntàta
Dadaidh agus An Càr
Oidhche Gheamhraidh

As A' Bhiobull series published by Acair 1980.
Stories from the Bible translated into Gaelic by one of the team members,
Christina Mackenzie:
Gideon
Moire, Mathair Iosa
Rut
Peadar, An t-Iasgair
Original texts by Carinne Mackenzie. Illustrations by Mackay Design
Associates Ltd.

Gaelic adaptation of 'Breakthrough to Literacy' pupil's folder
Na Facail
Published by Longman for the Western Isles Islands Council 1980.
Original text by David Mackay and Brian Thompson. Longman 1970.

B.   ORIGINAL POEMS PUBLISHED IN BBC SCHOOLS
BOOKLETS.
Cladaichean
Tha làn an dràsd ann,
Faochagan
An Fhaoileag
Trosg agus adag
Gille agus iasg
Thuirt am bradan
Chuir mi ...
Nuair bhitheas dithean beag a' fàs
A' buain na monach
Nach bochd
Chaidh sinn a bhuain na monach (oran)
Uisge fiadhaich
Uisge a' tuiteam
Uisge
Curran is càl
Cuiridh sinn ...

C. POSTERS TO ACCOMPANY BBC SCHOOLS PROGRAMMES.

Domhnall MacDhomhnaill MacDhomhnaill to accompany the programmes "Fàs is Fallaineachd" broadcast in the BBC Scotland Schools radio series *Co Iad?* 1977. Drawing by Andrew McMorrine.

An t-Udal to accompany the archaeological unit of programmes broadcast in the BBC Scotland Schools radio series *Co Iad?* 1977.

D. BOOKS DISTRIBUTED TO SCHOOLS AND PLAYGROUPS WITH GAELIC TEXT OVERLAID ON EXISTING TEXT.

An t-Snèip Mhòr Mhilis Chruinn.   *Corduroi*
Tarmod agus am Peana Purpaidh.   *Aon, Dhà, Trì*
Cuileanan a' Fàs Mòr.   *Mach 's a Steach*
Am Balach Beag agus an t-Each.   *Balach Beag agus Curran Mor*
Deise Ur a' Phaidein.   *Rob agus a' Chlach Dhearg*
An t-Iasg Seunta.   *Tigh Sheumais*
Coig Iseanan Beaga.   *Ruairidh*
Domhnull Ruadh.   *Aonghas a' dol a Chadal*
    Spotan an Cù Salach

Gaelic adaptations by project team and others, edited by project team.

E. MATERIALS DISTRIBUTED TO SCHOOLS, UNPUBLISHED.

Na Facail
Word book to accompany the Gaelic adaptation of "Breakthrough to Literacy."

Say It In Gaelic Poster to accompany the BBC Scotland Gaelic School Radio Series *Say It In Gaelic* broadcast in 1980. Drawing by Katharine Barr.

Eun Gràineil a' Bhagh Mhòr
Aig a' Chladach
Aig an Abhainn
Aig an Fhang
Aig a' Chidhe
A' dol gu Eirisgeidh
Na Bocsaichean Arain

Sùilean Dubha
Cassette of Gaelic rhymes and songs produced in conjunction with the Community Education Project.

Am Foghar
Iasgach
Thematic Sequences of enlarged B/W photographs.

Early Reading series trial material
anns an sgoil   *bàtaichean*
na cearcan ùra   *dadai ag iasgach*
na h-uain   *aig a' van*
an teaghlach againn   *a'dol do'n sgoil*

Original Illustrated Booklets
An Cu aig Muir   *Ag Iasgach*
Teddi agus an Luchag   *Am Bodach Feannaig*
An Kite   *Coig Luchain Bheaga*
Luchag anns an Arbhar   *Luch aig an Uinneig*
An Cat Dubh Agam   *Sloc Bhuntata*
Niall air a' Chladach   *Luchain Tigh Mairi*
An t-Ubhal Agam

Guidance Notes for Selected Topics
An Traigh   *Sinn Fhéin*
Uisge   *Am Foghar*
Rudan a théid a Chur   *Am Baile*
Móine   *Planadh agus Mapadh*
Caoraich agus Uain   *Aiseagan*
Eòin   *Cànan*
An Geamhradh

Guidance Notes for a Work of Fiction as Centre of Interest
Tugainn Cuairt   *Sula*
Hill's End   *Stig of the Dump*
Mark of the Horselord   *Horned Helmet*
Uilleam Bàn   *Rònan agus Brianuilt*
Boy with the Bronze Axe *Spàgan*

Appendix 3

PROJECT SCHOOLS 1975-81

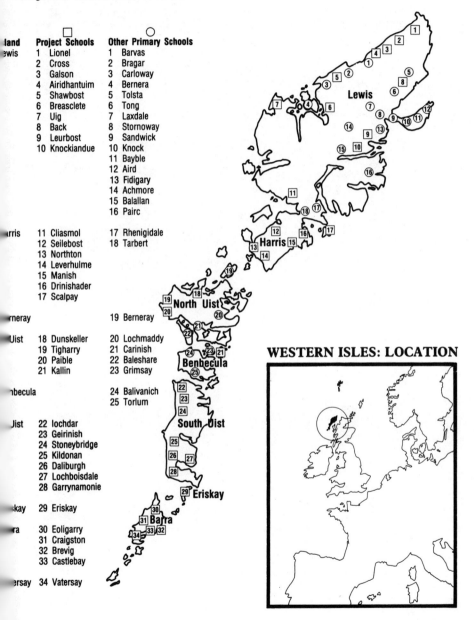

	Project Schools		Other Primary Schools
Island			
Lewis	1 Lionel	1	Barvas
	2 Cross	2	Bragar
	3 Galson	3	Carloway
	4 Airidhantuim	4	Bernera
	5 Shawbost	5	Tolsta
	6 Breasclete	6	Tong
	7 Uig	7	Laxdale
	8 Back	8	Stornoway
	9 Leurbost	9	Sandwick
	10 Knockiandue	10	Knock
		11	Bayble
		12	Aird
		13	Fidigary
		14	Achmore
		15	Balallan
		16	Pairc
Harris	11 Cliasmol	17	Rhenigidale
	12 Seilebost	18	Tarbert
	13 Northton		
	14 Leverhulme		
	15 Manish		
	16 Drinishader		
	17 Scalpay		
Berneray		19	Berneray
N Uist	18 Dunskeller	20	Lochmaddy
	19 Tigharry	21	Carinish
	20 Paible	22	Baleshare
	21 Kallin	23	Grimsay
Benbecula		24	Balivanich
		25	Torlum
S Uist	22 Iochdar		
	23 Geirinish		
	24 Stoneybridge		
	25 Kildonan		
	26 Daliburgh		
	27 Lochboisdale		
	28 Garrynamonie		
Eriskay	29 Eriskay		
Barra	30 Eoligarry		
	31 Craigston		
	32 Brevig		
	33 Castlebay		
Vatersay	34 Vatersay		

WESTERN ISLES: LOCATION